NORTON TEXTRA WRITER

WITH
ONLINE HANDBOOK

ACADEMIC CONSULTANT

Myron Tuman

University of Alabama

NORTON TEXTRA WRITER

WITH
ONLINE HANDBOOK

Ann Arbor Software

W · W · NORTON & COMPANY

New York · London

Manual revised by Myron Tuman and Don Langham.
Manual produced using Textra 6.0.

Manual copyright © 1992, 1989, 1988 by W. W. Norton & Company, Inc.
Word processing software copyright © 1992, 1991, 1990, 1989, 1988 by Ann Arbor
Software
Online handbook copyright © 1992, 1990, 1989, 1988 by W. W. Norton & Company,
Inc.
Textra is a registered trademark of Ann Arbor Software.

Printed in the United States of America

NORTON TEXTRA WRITER 2.5
Manual with two 5.25" disks   ISBN 0-393-96278-4
Manual with one 3.5" disk   ISBN 0-393-96277-6

NORTON TEXTRA WRITER 2.5 TO ACCOMPANY
THE CONFIDENT WRITER, SECOND EDITION
Manual with two 5.25" disks   ISBN 0-393-96257-1
Manual with one 3.5" disk   ISBN 0-393-96256-3

NORTON TEXTRA WRITER 2.5 TO ACCOMPANY
THE NORTON GUIDE TO WRITING
Manual with two 5.25" disks   ISBN 0-393-96263-6
Manual with one 3.5" disk   ISBN 0-393-96262-8

NORTON TEXTRA WRITER 2.5 TO ACCOMPANY
WRITING—A COLLEGE HANDBOOK, THIRD EDITION
Manual with two 5.25" disks   ISBN 0-393-96274-1
Manual with one 3.5" disk   ISBN 0-393-96273-3

W. W. Norton & Company, Inc., 500 Fifth Avenue, New York, New York 10110
W. W. Norton & Company, Ltd., 10 Coptic Street, London WC1A 1PU

1 2 3 4 5 6 7 8 9 0

Contents

v

Preface

Computers simplify. They make possible. With a computer's help, you can do many things more quickly; you can do other things that would be too complicated to do without their help. A paper neatly prepared on a typewriter seems like a final draft even when you identify improvements that could be made: it's just too much trouble to retype a whole paper. A paper prepared on a computer, on the other hand, invites revision; correcting typos, changing margins, shifting and reshaping paragraphs, and then printing the paper out again are quick and easy matters.

Too often, though, the software that is supposed to enable you to tap the power of computers isn't within your reach—either because it's too expensive or because it's so complicated that the benefits of using it are outweighed by the trouble or time of mastering it.

Norton Textra is priced within your budget and is so easy to use that you will spend your time writing, not mastering command codes or keyboard templates, or hopelessly searching a fat manual for the answer to your question.

This new version, 2.5, adds an alternate set of pull-down menus as well as full mouse support, making the program even easier to use—and more fun.

Most options are given onscreen in either traditional function-key or new pull-down menus. Frequently a general option leads to a new menu with more specific choices. Take your time (computers don't get impatient) and take some chances (almost all mistakes can be undone). Before you know it, using *Norton Textra* will be something you do without thinking about it; instead your mind will focus on you writing— on saying just what you want to say and saying it the most effective way you can.

NORTON TEXTRA WRITER

WITH
ONLINE HANDBOOK

1

Getting Started

1.1 An overview of *Norton Textra*

1.1.1 Where to start

As soon as you have *Norton Textra* up and running (see **1.2**), you should probably put this reference manual aside and work directly with the computer. Just as a manual on tennis is no substitute for time spent on the court, racket in hand, practicing swing and stroke, learning to react to the ball, this manual cannot replace your time at a computer, hands on the keyboard, writing and revising, saving and printing.

You should also begin to *write* — not just practice — as soon as you can, and you should write something that actually has meaning for you. If you begin with just a practice session, you are likely to spend a good deal of time learning commands you may never need, not remember very much of what you have learned, and be bored pretty quickly.

Instead, begin a paper that is due shortly. Or write a letter that you have been wanting to write. Or write a short story or a poem or the lyrics to a song that you've been trying to work out in your head. Concentrate on the *writing*, not on the *word processing*. Learn *Norton Textra* commands and procedures only as you need them.

At first, in fact, you will be using the keyboard very much as you would use a typewriter keyboard, typing words, phrases, sentences. You won't need to know much of anything special about *Norton Textra*. As you begin to change text — "My paper is about how computers are more trouble than they're worth" might become "Computers may be useful, but they're a lot of trouble" and then "Personal computers, despite their reputation for being too difficult for most of us, offer a lot of advantages

1

for even everyday writers like me"—you'll gradually learn how to insert and delete, how to move around both on the screen and to parts of your document not currently shown on the screen. You may not at first learn the very quickest ways to do what you want, but you can learn shortcuts later, as you gain confidence and experience. And there are things *not* to worry about: for example, you won't need the *Merge* command in your first document, so don't bother to learn it yet.

Remember that you are writing something you want or need to write; *Norton Textra* is nothing more than a tool to help you write and revise more quickly and easily than you otherwise could.

1.1.2 Help available on your diskette

Never forget that even with this reference manual stored on a shelf far from the computer you are using, your *Norton Textra* diskette itself offers plenty of help to get you through almost any difficulty.

If you want a brief introduction to the computer, to word processing, and to *Norton Textra*, you should call up the film-on-disk tutorials (see **2.4**), entertaining "filmstrips" that are shown right on your screen.

If you are ever in doubt about the options *Norton Textra* is offering you, you can press [Alt H] for help (see **2.6**). And if, while you are writing or revising a document, you need help with grammatical or rhetorical questions—questions about writing—you can press [F5] (see **4.6**).

1.1.3 The reference manual

You will probably find that you can happily and profitably use *Norton Textra* without ever referring to this manual. There are at least two situations, however, where it might come in handy.

If you simply cannot understand a given command or option, even with the onscreen help, you can use the manual's index to find a concise explanation here.

After you have mastered the basics of *Norton Textra*, you may want to browse through this manual to see what other capabilities the program offers that you haven't already discovered.

1.1.4   Five basic activities of word processing

Word processing with *Norton Textra* consists of five basic activities:

1. *Creating* a new document, or retrieving a previously prepared document. This is discussed in chapter 2.

2. *Editing* the document, which refers both to entering text and to revising it by adding or deleting, rearranging blocks of text, etc. This is discussed in chapters 3–6.

3. *Formatting* a document so that it will look the way you want when you print it out. *Norton Textra* is set up to make basic formatting decisions for you, so formatting will be a separate activity only when you want to do things differently. Formatting is discussed in chapter 7.

4. *Printing* all or part of the document. This is discussed in chapter 8.

5. *Saving* the changed document onto a disk. This is discussed in chapter 9.

1.2   Starting *Norton Textra*

If you are working on a computer in a writing lab or computer center, you should follow the instructions you are given. Such a computer may be set up for you so that you can begin working directly with *Norton Textra*. In other cases, the following instructions will prove useful.

You cannot start a personal computer with your *Norton Textra* disk alone, but must instead begin with DOS. Insert a DOS diskette into the A drive (usually the left-hand or top drive) of your computer and turn on the power. You may be prompted to enter the date and time. When you have responded, the DOS prompt

$$A >\_$$

will appear on the screen. This signifies that the A disk drive is the default drive and that DOS is ready to do your bidding.

Remove the DOS disk from the A drive and replace it with your *Norton Textra* Program disk. (You should always use a backup copy of your *Norton Textra* disk, NOT the original. See **1.3** for instructions on how to make a backup.)

With the DOS prompt (A > _) on the screen, type **norton** and press [Enter]. The disk drive will spin for about ten seconds while *Norton Textra* is loaded into memory, the screen will clear, and then the *Norton Textra* copyright screen will appear, followed by the *Opening menu* (see **2.2**).

1.3   Making a backup copy of *Norton Textra*

Copying *Norton Textra* for the use of others is illegal, as spelled out in the licensing agreement on the copyright page. But, for the sake of safety, you should make a copy for your own use and store the original in a safe place. The steps for doing this are listed below. There are two sets of instructions—one for systems with a single floppy-disk drive and one for those with two or more floppy-disk drives.

1.3.1   Preparation

You'll need a blank disk that you can use for the backup copy. You'll also need a *DOS disk*—the disk that came with the computer you are using or a copy of that disk.

Your computer should be on, the DOS prompt A > _ should be on the screen, and the DOS disk should be in the A disk drive.

1.3.2   Instructions for systems with one floppy disk drive

1. Type **DISKCOPY** and press [Enter].
2. The message

> `Insert source disk in drive A:`
> `Press any key . . .`

will appear. Note: If the message **Bad command or filename** appears, you'll need to insert the DOS disk that contains the DISKCOPY program. Remove the disk in drive A, put the *Norton Textra* Program disk into the drive, and press any key. The message

> `Reading . . .`

will appear while DOS reads the disk.

3. After the disk has been read, the message

> `Insert target disk in drive B:`
> `Strike any key when ready`

will appear. Remove the *Norton Textra* Program disk and replace it with the blank disk. Now press any key. DOS will begin copying onto the (previously) blank disk. If the blank disk was unformatted, the message

> `Formatting while copying . . .`

will appear. Otherwise, no message will appear. If there is enough memory in the system, DOS will be able to complete the copying in one step, and will move directly to step 4. If there isn't enough memory, DOS will cycle back to step 2, and instruct you to

> `Insert source diskette in drive A:`

You will need to remove the previously blank disk and replace it with the *Norton Textra* Program disk, as described in step 2. You will cycle through steps 2 and 3 until the copying is complete (usually 2 or 3 cycles).

4. When the copying is completed, the message

> `Copy complete`
> `Copy another (Y/N)?`

will appear. Press [N] to return to the DOS prompt.

1.3.3 Instructions for systems with two or more floppy disk drives

1. Type **DISKCOPY A: B:** and press [Enter].

2. The message

   > **Insert source diskette in drive A:**
   > **Insert target diskette in drive B:**
   >
   > **Strike any key when ready**

   will appear. Note: If the message **Bad command or filename** appears, you'll need to insert the DOS disk that contains the DISKCOPY program. Remove your DOS disk, and be careful to put the *Norton Textra* Program disk into drive A and the blank disk into drive B. (If you reverse the disks you'll end up with two blank ones.) Now press any key. The message

   Copying 9 sectors per track, 2 side(s)

   will appear while DOS copies the disk. If the disk you're copying onto is unformatted, the message

   > **Formatting while copying**

   will also appear. When the copying is completed, the message

   > **Copy complete**
   > **Copy another (Y/N)?**

   will appear. Press [N] to return to the DOS prompt.

1.3.4 Possible errors in the backup procedure

There are several errors that could occur during this backup procedure. If the computer beeps, and the message

> **Unrecoverable verify error on target**
> **Track xx, Sector x**
> **Target disk may be unusable**

appears, it means the disk you're trying to copy onto is bad. Try another disk.

If the computer beeps, and the message

```
Unrecoverable verify error on source
Track xx, Sector x
```

appears, it might mean that the program disk has gone bad during the shipping process.

If you have a defective disk, you can get a replacement copy by mailing the original disk back to

> W. W. Norton & Company, Inc.
> 500 Fifth Avenue
> New York, NY 10110
> Attention: Norton Textra

Be sure to enclose your return address with the defective disk.

1.4   Creating a self-booting *Norton Textra* disk

If you are working with one or two floppy disk drives, you may wonder why you have to bother with two diskettes – DOS and *Norton Textra*. You have to load DOS each time you want to start up your computer, then remove the DOS disk (or change disk drives) and, finally, type **norton** to load *Norton Textra*. You may wonder if there isn't an easier way.

And there is. You can create a self-booting disk – a disk that includes the essential parts of both DOS and *Norton Textra*. You can put such a disk into the computer you are using, turn on the computer, and both DOS and *Norton Textra* will be loaded automatically.

1.4.1   Formatting with system files

Section **1.3** explains how to make a backup copy of *Norton Textra*. If you have already made such a backup, you will find some of the following steps similar to instructions there.

You'll need a blank disk that you can use for the self-booting disk. You'll also need the DOS disk that came with the computer you are using or a copy of that disk.

The computer should be on, the DOS prompt A> should be on the screen, and the DOS disk should be in the A drive.

Instructions for systems with one floppy disk drive

1. Type **format /s** and press [Enter].

2. The message

    Insert new diskette for drive A:
    and strike any key when ready

    will appear. Remove the DOS disk from drive A, put the blank disk in the drive, and press any key. The message

    Formatting...

    will appear.

3. After the disk has been formatted, you will see something like the following (the numbers may be somewhat different):

    Formatting...Format complete
    System transferred

    362496 bytes total disk space
    40960 bytes used by system
    321536 bytes available on disk

    Format another (Y/N)?

    Press [N] to return to the DOS prompt A>.

Instructions for systems with two or more floppy disk drives

1. Type **format b:/s** and press [Enter].

2. The message

```
Insert new diskette for drive B:
and strike any key when ready
```

will appear. Put the blank disk in the drive, and press any key. The message

```
Formatting...
```

will appear.

3. After the disk has been formatted, you will see something like the following (the numbers may be somewhat different):

```
Formatting...Format complete
System transferred

   362496 bytes total disk space
    40960 bytes used by system
   321536 bytes available on disk

Format another (Y/N)?
```
Press [N] to return to the DOS prompt A>.

1.4.2   Copying the essential *Norton Textra* files

The DOS system files you have just transferred will take up nearly 41,000 bytes on your new disk. If you use a 3½" disk, there should be room for the DOS system files and all the *Norton Textra* files.

This is not the case if you use a 5¼" disk. You will need to leave off your self-booting diskette one of the help files (one of the files with the extension .HLP). There are two: NORTON.HLP, which contains the onscreen help (**2.6**); and HANDBOOK.HLP (**4.6**).

The one essential file to copy is NORTON.EXE.

1. At the DOS prompt, type **copy norton.exe b:** and press [Enter].

2. You will be told to

> **Insert diskette for drive B: and**
> **strike any key when ready**

Put your disk, formatted with system files (**1.4.1**), into drive A (if you have only one disk drive) or drive B (if you have two or more) and press [Enter].

3. You will know that the file has been copied successfully when you are told

> **1 File(s) copied.**

You need to use this copy command for each file you copy. You should now copy the .HLP files you have room for, as discussed above.

1.4.3   Making an AUTOEXEC.BAT file

Place your new disk in drive A. At the A> prompt, type

> **copy con autoexec.bat**

and press [Enter]. Then type **norton** and press [F6]. On the screen, ^Z will appear; press [Enter].

This creates an *autoexec.bat* file—a *bat*ch file that follows certain commands (*exec*utes) *auto*matically. DOS will look for this file and carry out the instructions you have left—the *norton* command tells DOS to load the NORTON.EXE file.

When you boot your computer with this new disk, DOS and *Norton Textra* will both load automatically.

1.5   Strategies for using *Norton Textra* on different systems

1.5.1   Systems with one floppy disk drive

When you are word processing on systems with a single floppy disk drive you can proceed in either of two ways.

Using a program/data disk

You can keep your *Norton Textra* program files and your documents all on one disk. This has the benefit of being easy to use and it cuts down on disk shuffling, but it limits the amount of space on your disk for documents. (Since *Norton Textra* allows you to switch disks if the current disk becomes full, this isn't as bad as it seems.)

If you use this approach you will probably want to maximize the available room on your program/data disk. One way to get more room for your own files is to delete the film-on-disk tutorials from your program/data disk. (But remember: you should be using a backup program disk, not the original.) Once you have become familiar with *Norton Textra*, you may not need these filmstrips on your working disk, so you can tell *Norton Textra* to delete FILM.HLP.

Using separate program and data disks

You can keep a *Norton Textra* Program disk and a separate, formatted data disk. Start *Norton Textra* as described in **1.2**. After *Norton Textra* is loaded and the *Opening* menu is displayed, press [R] to reach the *Retrieve document* menu. Remove the program disk and place your data disk (which must be a formatted disk; see **B.3.6**) in the disk drive. Now, select the *[F5]/Change disk drive* command. When *Norton Textra* prompts you to select the new disk drive, press [A] and *Norton Textra* will list the documents on the new disk. You can now select a document or create a new one, and begin editing.

This method allows you to have more documents on one disk, and it has some organizational benefits as well. While you need just one program disk, you may want several data disks, grouped according to your needs—one data disk for personal files, for example, and one for schoolwork; or one for English, one for sociology, one for engineering.

1.5.2   Systems with two floppy disk drives

Having two floppy disk drives essentially eliminates the decision outlined above. You can place the *Norton Textra* Program disk in drive A, and a data disk in drive B.

After starting *Norton Textra*, select the *[F5]/Change disk drive* command from the *Retrieve document* menu. When you're prompted to enter the disk drive letter, press [B]. *Norton Textra* will switch to drive B and list the documents on that disk. You can now select a document or create a new one, and begin editing.

1.5.3   Using Norton Textra on hard disk systems

Make your hard disk the current drive by switching over to C: (or D:), so that the C> (or D>) prompt is on the screen. Place the *Norton Textra* Program disk in drive A.

If you use sub-directories, create a sub-directory for *Norton Textra*. Type

MD TEXTRA

and press [Enter]. (You can, of course, choose a name other than Textra if you like.) Next, change over to that sub-directory by typing

CD \TEXTRA

Now you can put the *Norton Textra* Program disk in drive A, and type

COPY A:*.*

DOS will now copy all the files onto your hard disk. (The asterisks are explained in **2.5.14**.)

If you don't use sub-directories, just copy all the files from the *Norton Textra* Program disk onto your hard disk using the COPY command shown above.

If you have purchased *Norton Textra* on a 3½" disk you need to copy *.* only a single time. The 5¼" version, however, comes on two disks; you should copy both onto your hard disk.

2

Creating or
Retrieving a Document

2.1   Dealing with documents

Before the appearance of personal computers, most college
students did not worry too much about a system for keeping track
of their documents. Papers were begun on whatever writing
material was handy, stuck in a notebook for safekeeping, later
typed from rough notes, and, when returned, stuck in a drawer
where years later they might again come to light.

Since in word processing, text files are stored as magnetic
impulses, you need a more systematic method of dealing with
documents; you can't move these magnetic impulses around with
your hands. Thus, to do with a word processing program what
you have always done in writing a paper you need some common
procedures and common language.

Specifically, you have to learn three basic functions:

1. Creating a document (including how to name it)
2. Saving a document
3. Retrieving it (in order to work with it some more).

In addition, there are a number of somewhat less important
but still common tasks you will want to perform, such as
copying, deleting, and renaming documents, and working with
the disk drives and directories so that you can reach the
documents you want.

2.2   The Opening menu

After you have started *Norton Textra* (see **1.2**) the *Opening* menu will appear on the screen, as shown below:

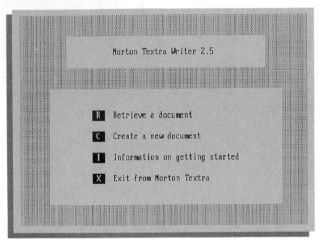

This menu offers you four options to choose among: to retrieve an existing document; to create a new document; to obtain more information about *Norton Textra*; or to exit from *Norton Textra* and return to DOS. A fifth option (to press [Alt H] for help) is available to you at all times within *Norton Textra*.

2.3   Creating a new document

If you press [C] from the *Opening* menu, *Norton Textra* will take you to the blank screen of a new, unnamed document. After you have written as much as you wish during this work session, you can save your document (**3.2.3**), and *Norton Textra* will ask you to name the document at that time:

**This document is unnamed, and
needs to be named before saving.**

Enter file name : _

Guidelines for naming documents are given in **2.4**.

If the name you enter is already being used on that disk (or directory), *Norton Textra* will prompt you

There is already a document named

xxxxxx.xxx

Do you want to overwrite it ? _
([Y] or [N], [Esc] to cancel)

You can also create a new document simply by typing the name you want to give it in the *Retrieve document* menu and then pressing [Enter]. The following boxed message will appear:

Document wasn't found.
Do you want to create it ([Y] or [N]) ?

Press [N] to cancel or [Y] to create the document.

2.4   Naming documents

Document names consist of a *filename* (1 to 8 characters long) and an optional *extension* (1 to 3 characters long). The filename is the basic name of your document; the extension, if you want to use one, can help you identify the type of document (you might use it to identify the course for which the document is intended: BIO, PSY, ENG). The characters you use must be letters (A–Z), numbers (0–9), or any of the following:

$$ \$ \ \& \ \# \ @ \ ! \ \% \ ' \ ` \ (\ ) \ - \ \{ \ \} $$

SPACES ARE NOT ALLOWED, so if you want to separate elements in a filename use a hyphen.
Some sample filenames are shown below:

HAMLET	(filename, no extension)
REPORT.BIO	(filename + extension)
NURSING.1	(filename + extension)

TO-DAD.$$$ (filename + extension)

The filename and extension should be descriptive enough of the contents of the document that you will be able to find quickly the particular file you want. **NURSING.1**, **NURSING.2**, and **NURSING.3** would be useful names if they represent notes on those chapters in your text or clear divisions of a research report. But more descriptive or distinctive names would be better if you find yourself never remembering just what is in which **NURSING** file.

While *Norton Textra* displays document names in directories like this:

`SAMPLE    LET`

you must type the filename and extension next to each other, with a period in between, like this:

`SAMPLE.LET`

2.5   Retrieve a document

2.5.1   The *Retrieve document* menu

If you press [R] from the *Opening* menu, the *Retrieve document* menu will appear on the screen:

```
    Current directory is A:                    Documents        Size

                                          1 - BIOLOGY    1      3,905
                                          2 - HEMINGWY   ENG   12,158
                                          2 - PAPER      DOC    7,964
    Directory commands                    4 - TO-DAD     $$$    1,870

F1 - Display recently edited documents        End of directory
F2 - Directory listing commands
F4 - Display disk free space - Off
F5 - Change disk drive

    Document commands

F6 - Copy
F7 - Print
F8 - Delete
F9 - Rename



            Retrieve document : [Esc] to exit, [Alt H] for help

            Enter document name or number : _
```

2.5.2   The document directory

The right side of the screen lists the *documents* (or *files*) on the current disk drive and indicates the size of each in bytes. This list is called a *directory*. If there are more than sixteen documents on the disk, the message

[PgUp], [PgDn] for more

will be displayed at the bottom of the directory, and you can press [PgDn] and [PgUp] to move forward and backward through the list of documents.

The message **End of directory** will appear when the last document has been displayed. If you press [PgDn] when this message is on the screen, *Norton Textra* will go to the beginning of the directory, and list the first sixteen files again. Note: subdirectories are listed along with files. To change to a directory, enter the number next to it. To move to a parent directory, enter the number next to . . (dir)

2.5.3   Retrieving an existing document

You can retrieve a document from the *Retrieve document* menu by typing either its name or the number next to it in the onscreen directory. If the document you want to retrieve is not listed on the screen (because there are more than sixteen documents on the disk or in the directory), you can still retrieve it by name, but to retrieve it by number you will have to use [PgDn] or [PgUp] until it appears onscreen. (Or you can use *shorthand document retrieval*, **2.5.6.**)

After you have typed the name or number of the document to be edited and pressed [Enter], the message

Reading in document . . .

will appear while *Norton Textra* retrieves the document. Then the document you've retrieved will appear on the screen, ready for editing.

2.5.4   Shortcut for creating or retrieving a document

If you know the name of the document you want to work on, you can type it in at the same time you type **norton** at the DOS prompt at the beginning of your work session. Skip a space after **norton**, type the filename, and press [Enter]:

norton filename

The *Retrieve document* menu will be skipped, and the document will be read in directly. If you are creating a document, you will be told that the document wasn't found and asked if you want to create it.

You can use this shortcut even to retrieve a document that is on a different drive or in a different directory. Type **norton**, skip a space, and then type the drive letter, a colon, and the filename:

norton b:mobydick

Or type the drive letter, a backslash, the directory name, backslash, and filename:

norton c:\papers\mobydick

In either case, press [Enter] afterwards.

2.5.5   F1 - *Display recently edited documents*

This command allows you to retrieve documents quickly. It lists both the documents you have retrieved most recently in that work session and the documents you have recently merged from. Next to each document name is a letter; simply push the corresponding key to open the document.

2.5.6   F2 - *Directory listing commands*

This command gives you control over what *Norton Textra* lists in directories and how.

Directory listing commands menu

When you press [F1], the following menu will appear:

```
                                           Documents        Size

 F2 - Sort directories - By name         1 - BIOLOGY   1      3,905
 F3 - Preserve original format - Off     2 - HEMINGWY  ENG   12,158
 F4 - Shorthand document retrieval - Off 2 - PAPER     DOC    7,964
                                         4 - TO-DAD    $$$    1,870

     Documents to highlight in directory     End of directory

 A - *.LET      B - Off        C - Off


     Documents NOT to list in directory

 D - *.EXE      H - *.WRD      L - Off
 E - *.HLP      I - *.DRV      M - Off
 F - *.COM      J - *.NOV      N - Off
 G - *.BAK      K - Off        O - Off



       Directory listing commands : [Esc] to exit, [Alt H] for help

            Select command : _
```

F2 - Sort directories

If this command is off, filenames in the directory will be presented to you simply in the order that DOS has catalogued them on your disk. While this order may make sense to DOS, *you* may find it more useful to reorder the directory to find documents more readily.

Pressing [F2] allows you to have *Norton Textra* present files to you by name, by extension, or by date/time:

```
N - By name
E - By extension
D - By date/time
O - Off

Select choice : _
```

By name will list your files alphabetically by filename. (See also *shorthand document retrieval* below.)

By extension will list your files alphabetically by extension (see **2.4** for an explanation of filenames and extensions); those files with no filename extensions will be listed first, alphabetically by filename. Listing files this way will be useful if you have given similar files the same extension: all letters **.LET**, for example, or all your biology notes .BIO.

By date/time will list your files chronologically by the date and time you last retrieved them, beginning with the most recent. The use of this sorting method depends on the correct date and time being kept by your computer's clock or by your entering the correct date and time when you boot the computer.

Off returns the order of filenames in directories to the DOS order. It will take *Norton Textra* slightly longer to display directories if they're sorted.

F3 - Preserve original format

This switch should be left on if you want *Norton Textra* to save your documents in their original format.

F4 - Shorthand document retrieval

If your directory is being sorted by name (see above), this command will help you deal with a large number of documents on a disk or in a subdirectory. (If *Sort directories* is not already switched to *By name*, pushing [F4] will make this change.)

If you want to retrieve a document called RESEARCH, for example, typing the R will move quickly through the directory so that the first document listed will be the first document whose name begins with *r*. If that document is the one you want, press [1] and [Enter] and you will be placed in the document. If your document is listed third, press [3], [Enter]; or if it is listed tenth, press [1] [0], [Enter]. Or you can type RE or RES, and so forth, thereby changing the directory, until document number one in the directory is the one you want or until that document shows up in the onscreen directory.

This shortcut will be especially useful if your documents have names that might easily be mistyped, such as RES1989.QYZ.

Documents to highlight in directories

You can highlight certain documents in your directory listings in bold in order to make them easier to find. For example, if you select *.BIO in this command (see **2.5.14** on global filename characters), *Norton Textra* will highlight document names ending in .BIO when it lists directories.

To highlight such files, press one of the letters offered, [B] for example. You will be prompted to enter extension. The asterisk (*) and period will already be on the screen; you just type BIO, and this extension will replace the **Off** after the **B** above.

If you decide no longer to highlight files with the extensions listed, simply press the letter beside that extension to turn the highlighting off.

Documents NOT to list in directories

You can also tell *Norton Textra* not to list certain documents in directory listings. For example, *.BAK here condenses your directory listings by not listing backup files, *.EXE, by not listing program files that you would not want to edit anyway.
You can add or delete extensions here as you do in *Documents to highlight*, explained just above.

2.5.7   F4 - *Display disk free space*

If this switch is on, the amount of space left on the current disk drive will be displayed at the end of the directory listing. Directories will take slightly longer to list if this switch is on.

2.5.8   F5 - *Change disk drive*

When you press [F5] you will be prompted to **Select disk drive**. Just above the prompt *Norton Textra* will indicate what disk drives are available and, at the top left of the screen, the current drive and subdirectory. Press the letter of the drive you want. The screen will be updated to show you the new drive letter and a directory of the documents on that drive or subdirectory. (You can also change directories by using the direct DOS command; see **2.5.13**.)

2.5.9   F6 - *Copy*

This command allows you to make an exact copy of a document. *Norton Textra* will ask for the document you want copied by prompting

Enter document name or number : _

When you have replied, you will be asked

Where do you want to copy it : _

Type the name you want to give the copy. If you enter the name of an existing document here, *Norton Textra* will overwrite that document with the new copy.

2.5.10 F7 - *Print*

This command allows you to print a document without first retrieving it. (But note that this command will print one copy of the entire document as it is currently formatted; if you want to print more than one copy with a single command, or just part of the document, or change the format, you must retrieve the document. See chapter 8 for more about printing.) You will be prompted to

Enter document name or number : _

After you select a document, *Norton Textra* will prompt you to

Press any key to begin printing... _
(Press [Esc] if you change your mind)

2.5.11 F8 - *Delete*

This command allows you to throw away a document (or a specific copy of a document) you are finished with. You will be prompted to

Enter document name or number : _

You can enter either a single document name or number or a wildcard name (such as *.BAK; see **2.5.14** on global filename characters).

Norton Textra will always ask you to confirm documents about to be deleted:

```
Document to be deleted : XXXXXX.XXX
Delete it ([Y] or [N], [Esc] to cancel) ? _
```

This gives you a chance to change your mind.

2.5.12 F9 - *Rename*

You will be prompted to

```
Enter document name or number : _
```

Enter the name of the document you want to rename. *Norton Textra* will then prompt you to

```
Enter new document name : _
```

Type in the new name you want to give the document. You can press [Esc] to cancel this command.

2.5.13 Direct DOS commands

Norton Textra also allows you to type the DOS commands CD, CHDIR, DEL, ERASE, and DIR directly in both the *Retrieve document* and the *Directory commands* menus. (See appendix B for an explanation of these commands.)

In addition, you can switch disk drives as in DOS by typing the drive letter and a colon (e.g., A:).

2.5.14 Global filename characters

The question mark (?) and the asterisk (*) can be used as shortcuts when referring to files already named. They are called global filename characters or wildcards.

A question mark (?) used in a filename or extension indicates that any single character can occupy that position. NURSING.?, for example, can indicate NURSING.1, NURSING.3,

NURSING.X. PAPER?.ENG can indicate PAPER1.ENG, PAPERS.ENG, and so forth.

An asterisk (called star) used in a filename or extension indicates that any character can occupy that position or any following position in the filename or the extension. The wildcard name *.LET, for example, refers to all documents with the filename extension LET. NURSING.* refers to all documents with the filename NURSING, no matter what extension.

A wildcard allows you to specify many documents with a single name. At the end of your nursing course, for instance, you could delete all nursing files from your working disk by typing **NURSING.*** at the delete prompt instead of typing each filename separately. You can quickly copy or delete all files in a directory with the command *.* which is called "star dot star."

2.5.15 Retrieving files in *WordPerfect 5* Format

Norton Textra will read *WordPerfect 5* files as if they were created using *Norton Textra*. In order for the conversion to work, the *Norton Textra* file WP5IN.NOV and the DOS file COMMAND.COM must be on the current disk or in the current pathname. If the message **Error running conversion** appears, chances are *Norton Textra* could not find one of these essential files. The same message will appear if insufficient memory is available to hold the file. See **9.9** for details about saving in *WordPerfect* format.

2.6   Using the help system

2.6.1   Information on getting started

If you press [I] from the *Opening* menu, the following screen will appear.

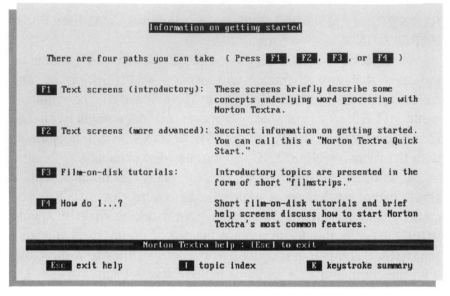

From here, you can choose any of the four paths described, each of which is designed to present introductory material on *Norton Textra* in a different way, to answer the needs of writers with different experience levels. You can experiment with each of these paths to find the one most useful to you.

If you press [F3], the menu that appears will allow you to select from among *Norton Textra*'s "film-on-disk" tutorials. These tutorials are similar to short film clips. They roll by on the screen, teaching you about *Norton Textra* through the use of pictures and examples. You can change speeds, fast forward, or rewind the film.

Seven commands help you use the film-on-disk tutorials:

F1   **Return to document** returns you to your document in the same place you were when you first asked for help.

F2   **Return to help screen** returns you to the help screen that was being displayed when you started the tutorial.

F3   **Restart this tutorial** rewinds the tutorial to the beginning and starts playing it again.

F5   Pause freezes the tutorial. The message **Press any key to resume** will appear to remind you how to restart the tutorial. Note that the tutorial might not freeze instantly – it won't freeze until the current activity (drawing a picture, for example) has been completed.

F6   Fast forward plays the tutorial at maximum speed. You can tap the [F6] key any time the tutorial is moving too slowly.

F7   Slow down decreases the speed of the tutorial. You can press [F7] several times if the tutorial is rolling by too quickly for you to read it comfortably.

F8   Speed up increases the speed of the tutorial slightly. Pressing it repeatedly will continue to increase the speed until it reaches its maximum.

2.6.2   Press [Alt H] any time you need some help

Whenever you have a question while using *Norton Textra*, press [Alt H] for help. *Norton Textra* will display a help screen for you – a screen full of text that describes the current command or menu. Help screens often lead to other help screens describing related topics in more detail.

   Norton Textra's help is *context-sensitive*. If you press [Alt H] when in you're in the *Search* command, for example, you'll get a help screen discussing the *Search* command. If you press [Alt H] while editing, you'll get the following table of contents of the help system:

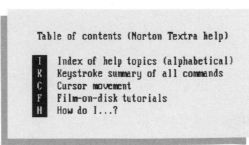

```
Table of contents (Norton Textra help)

   I    Index of help topics (alphabetical)
   K    Keystroke summary of all commands
   C    Cursor movement
   F    Film-on-disk tutorials
   H    How do I...?
```

[I]/Index of help topics provides easy access to all parts of the help system. *[K]/Keystroke summary of all commands* serves as an online reference card or template. *[C]/Cursor movement* summarizes the means of quickly moving to all parts of the screen or document. *[F]/Film-on-disk tutorials* takes students to a menu of filmstrips described in **2.6.1**. *[H]/How do I...?* provides quick answers to commonly asked questions.

2.7 Exit from *Norton Textra*

This is the command to choose when you're done with *Norton Textra* and want to run another program or leave the computer altogether.

3

Editing a Document

Two menu systems

Norton Textra has two separate menu systems: the traditional function key menus (described in detail in this and following chapters) and a new set of pull-down menus designed to be used with a mouse (described in chapter 10). To change menu systems manually, see **6.7.5**.

3.1   The editor

Once you've created or retrieved a document, you will be in the editing portion of *Norton Textra*, or *editor*. The editor allows you to insert or delete text, highlight it, or reformat it. You can also call upon other commands, such as *Print* or *Save*, from the editor.

The top line of the screen is the *status line*. It lists, at left, the name of the current document and, at right, your location in that document by page (including the line and column on that page). You can turn the status line off if you wish (see **6.7.5**).

The second line of the screen is a formatting ruler, showing margins and tabs.

The middle twenty lines of the screen are used for displaying your document. Since your documents can be longer than twenty lines, you might think of the screen as a window through which you can view that much of your document at a time. You move through the document with the cursor moving keys and other commands (see **3.3**).

Near the bottom of the screen is a bar that identifies the current menu. It also reminds you that you can press [Esc] to exit the current menu or [Alt H] for help.

The bottom two lines of the screen are used to display the current editing menu, which reminds you what the function keys do. The function keys will act differently depending on what part of *Norton Textra* you're using, but you can always refer to the bottom lines of the screen as a guide.

3.2 *Norton Textra*'s function key menu system

3.2.1 The three editing menus

In the editor, the function keys [F2]-[F10] are used for commands, and the [F1] key is used for displaying menus. Pressing [F1] repeatedly will cycle through *Norton Textra*'s three editing menus (chapters 4-6 will discuss these in detail).

When you press [F1], the *Edit* menu will be replaced by the *Shift* menu. You can select any of the commands listed by pressing the appropriate function key. For example, you could select the *Copy block* command by pressing [F5]. (Or, from the *Edit* menu, you could also press either [Shift] key plus the function key of the command you want [Shift F5], for example, to begin the *Copy block* command.)

If you press [F1] again, *Norton Textra*'s *Alt* menu will appear. You can select any of these commands by pressing the appropriate function key: [F4] for *Works cited*, for example. (Or, from the *Edit* menu, you could press [Alt F4].)

If you press [F1] yet again, you will return to the *Edit* menu.

3.2.2 Backing out of menus

Pressing the [Esc] key will back you out, one step at a time, from any path you've taken using *Norton Textra*'s menu system.

If you've started the *Print* command, for example, and you want to return to the editor, press [Esc]. Or, if you've already selected the *S - Print selected pages* option in the *Print* menu, *Norton Textra* will prompt you to

Start with page (between 1 and 1) : _

If you press [Esc] at this point, the prompt will disappear, and you will return to the *Print* menu, where you can select another option or press [Esc] again to return to the editor.

If you are several levels deep into menus, you can press [Esc] several times until you return to your document, or you can simply press [Ctrl F1]. No matter how deeply you've traveled into *Norton Textra*'s menus, pressing this express elevator combination will return you immediately to the editor.

If you press [Esc] at the *Edit* menu, you will move to the *Main* menu (**3.2.3**).

3.2.3   The *Main* menu

The *Main* menu is perhaps the most important menu in *Norton Textra*. You will use it every time you leave a document, whether or not you are saving the changes you have made, and whether you want to leave *Norton Textra* or to create or retrieve another document.

You reach the *Main* menu by pressing [Esc] from the *Edit* menu – that is, most of the time you are editing a document, you can simply press [Esc] a single time. If you are a level or more deep into the menu system, you can press [Esc] twice or more until you reach the *Main* menu.

The *Main* menu looks like this:

[S]/Save current document saves the current document onto disk, preserving any changes you may have made since the file was last saved or since it was created. (Chapter 9 talks more about saving.) Once the document is saved, you will still be at the *Main* menu, where you can choose one of the other options or press [Esc] to return to your document.

[P]/Print current document enables you to print the current document. You will be prompted to press any key to begin printing, or to press [Esc] if you change your mind. (Chapter 8 talks more about printing.) Once the document is printed, you will still be at the *Main* menu, where you can choose one of the other options or press [Esc] to return to your document.

[C]/Create a new document moves to the empty screen of a new document, just as in **2.3**. If, however, you have made changes to the current document, *Norton Textra* will first ask if you want to save those changes before creating a new document.

[R]/Retrieve a document takes you to a menu like the *Retrieve document* menu (**2.5.1**) where you can choose which document you wish to retrieve. If, however, you have made changes to the current document, *Norton Textra* will first ask if you want to save those changes before retrieving another document.

[X]/Exit from Norton Textra returns you to the DOS prompt. If, however, you have made changes to the current document, *Norton Textra* will first ask if you want to save those changes before exiting.

The keystrokes above are defined individually, but *Norton Textra* acts so quickly and your brain will learn the basic patterns so quickly that you'll probably soon find yourself using one or two sequences without waiting to read the *Main* menu. For example, to save your changes to a document and then retrieve another, you'll press [Esc],[S],[R]. Or, at the end of a writing session, to save your changes to a document and then exit from *Norton Textra*, you'll press [Esc],[S],[X]. The [Esc],[S] sequence is an important habit to get into, to keep from losing any changes you may have made.

3.3   Moving the cursor

3.3.1   The cursor keys

Moving the cursor—the blinking line you see on your screen—is a very important part of word processing, because this is how you tell *Norton Textra* where you want to make changes.

Norton Textra uses the special cursor moving keys on the right side of the IBM keyboard for moving the cursor. (If you're using an IBM-compatible computer, the keys may be differently located and labeled, but they should work in the same fashion.) These keys are shown below, along with the names that we'll use for them in this manual.

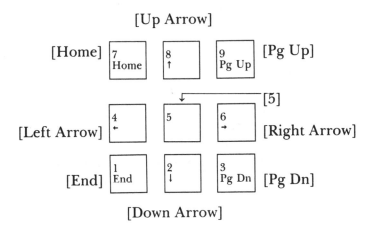

[NumLock]

Notice that most of the cursor moving keys have two things printed on them: a number and a cursor moving symbol (7 and Home, for example). This is because these keys can be used as a calculator-type keypad as well as cursor moving keys.

The [NumLock] key (located near the upper right corner of the IBM keyboard) toggles between the two abilities: each time you press the [NumLock] key, it will switch from number to symbol, or back again.

[Left Arrow], [Right Arrow]

These keys move the cursor left and right one character at a time. If the cursor is at the end of a line, pressing [Right Arrow] moves the cursor to the beginning of the next line. If the cursor is under the first character of a line, pressing [Left Arrow] moves the cursor to the end of the line above. (This system, called tightly tracking the text, is further described in **3.6**.)

[Up Arrow], [Down Arrow]

These keys move the cursor up or down one line. If the cursor is at the top (or bottom) of the screen, the text will scroll down (or up), and a new line will appear.

In moving from line to line, the cursor may appear to move erratically. Actually, it is moving quite logically; it will remain in the same column it began in, if there is text in that column. If there is no text in that column, the cursor will move left or right to the first text, but it will move back to the original column if in a succeeding line it finds text.

[Home], [End]

[Home] moves the cursor to the beginning of the current line. [End] moves to the end of the current line.

Pressing [Home] twice moves the cursor to the top of the screen. Pressing [Home] three times moves it to the beginning of the document.

Pressing [End] twice moves the cursor to the bottom of the screen. Pressing [End] three times moves it to the end of the document.

[PgUp], [PgDn]

These keys allow you to page through your text, one screen at a time. [PgUp] moves up to the previous screen full of text, and [PgDn] moves down to the next. There is a one-line overlap as you page through a document to help provide some continuity between screens of text.

3.3.2   Moving the cursor by word

The [Ctrl] key, in combination with [Left Arrow] or [Right Arrow], moves the cursor one word at a time.

[Ctrl Left Arrow]	Move to beginning of current word (or, if cursor is at beginning, to beginning of previous word)
[Ctrl Right Arrow]	Move to beginning of next word

In normal text, words are easily identifiable – they are separated by spaces. The following characters are treated the same as spaces:

,	(comma)
(	(left parentheses)
[	(left bracket)
.	(period or decimal point)

3.3.3   Moving the cursor by sentence

You can move to the beginning of the current sentence (or, if the cursor is already at the beginning, to the beginning of the previous sentence) or next sentence with the following cursor movers:

[Shift Left Arrow]   Move to beginning of current sentence (or, if cursor is at beginning, to beginning of previous sentence)

[Shift Right Arrow]   Move to beginning of next sentence

3.3.4 Moving the cursor by paragraph

You can move to the beginning of the current paragraph (or, if the cursor is already at the beginning, to the beginning of the previous paragraph) or next paragraph with the following cursor movers:

[Shift PgUp]   Move to beginning of current paragraph (or, if cursor is at beginning, to beginning of previous paragraph)

[Shift PgDn]   Move to beginning of next paragraph

3.3.5 Moving the cursor by printed page

[PgUp] and [PgDn] are oriented toward screen pages, but you can also move the cursor forward and backward by printed pages. (Remember that each screen full of text is less than a printed page of text.)

[Ctrl PgUp]   Move to top of current printed page (or, if cursor is at top, to top of previous printed page)

[Ctrl PgDn]   Move to top of next printed page

3.3.6   Moving to the beginning or end of a document

You can move to the beginning or end of your document with the following cursor movers:

[Ctrl Home]	Move to the beginning of the document
[Ctrl End]	Move to the end of the document

Remember that you can also move to the beginning of a document by pressing [Home] three times or to the end by pressing [End] three times.

3.4   *Go to* commands

3.4.1   Go to page, Go to line

[Alt P]	Go to page
[Alt G]	Go to line

You will be asked which page (or line) number you want to go to. If, for example, you press [Alt P] in a twelve-page document, you will be prompted to

Enter page number (between 1 and 12): _

If you enter a 2, *Norton Textra* will jump to the top of page 2.

3.4.2   Go to previous cursor position

[Ctrl G]	Go to previous cursor position

This command is especially useful in conjunction with bookmarks (see **3.5**) to allow you to jump back and forth quickly between two locations.

3.5   Bookmarks

A bookmark in *Norton Textra* allows you to leave an invisible marker anywhere in your text. You can then jump to the bookmark from anywhere else in your document.

3.5.1   Quick bookmarks

[Ctrl Q]	Sets the quick bookmark to the current cursor position
[Ctrl J]	Jumps to the quick bookmark

The quick bookmark allows you to set and jump to a marker with one keystroke. This is useful when you want to look at another section of your document, then return to the current location. Simply set the quick bookmark (nothing will happen on the screen), then go to the other section of your document. When you want to return, press [Ctrl J] to jump to the quick bookmark. (If nothing happens on the screen, either the quick bookmark has not been set or the cursor is already at the quick bookmark.)

3.5.2   Numbered bookmarks

[Alt Q]	Set numbered bookmark
[Alt J]	Jump to numbered bookmark

Norton Textra also provides nine numbered bookmarks. Although it takes two keystrokes to set or move to a numbered bookmark, there are nine of them available to you instead of just one as with the quick bookmark. The numbered bookmarks prove most useful when the locations will be jumped to frequently.

When you select either of these commands, you'll be prompted to

`Press bookmark number (1 through 9) : _`

After pressing one of the nine number keys (not function keys), *Norton Textra* will either set a bookmark at the current cursor position (if you pressed [Alt Q]), or jump to the numbered bookmark you selected (if you pressed [Alt J]). The cursor will not move if you select a numbered bookmark that has not been set.

3.6   Tightly tracking the text

You may be confused at first because you can't use the cursor moving keys to move into blank areas of the screen. For example, if the cursor is positioned on a blank line, as shown below,

```
Box 47
Fargo, ND   58100

Dear Mr. Smith,
```

and you press [Right Arrow], the cursor will move to the first character of the next line, like this:

```
Box 47
Fargo, ND   58100

Dear Mr. Smith,
```

This is called tightly tracking the text. After you've learned how it works you'll find it a fast way of moving the cursor around.

The cursor-moving keys can only move the cursor where there is existing text. Otherwise, use the [Spacebar], [Tab], [Enter], and [Backspace] keys.

When you create a new document, for example, the typing area is empty and the cursor is positioned at the paragraph margin of the first line, waiting for you to begin typing. At this point, no cursor movement is possible, since there isn't any text in the document. Pressing the cursor-moving keys will have no effect; the only thing you can do is insert text (or use [Spacebar], [Tab], or [Enter]).

1. If this is where you want to start the first line, go ahead and start typing.

2. If you want to start the first line a little further down, you can use the [Enter] key. The cursor will move down one line each time you press it, and on the screen it will look just as if you're moving the cursor using the [Down Arrow] key.

3. If you want to start the first line farther to the right, you can use the [Tab] or [Spacebar] keys. *Norton Textra* will insert spaces, and on the screen it will look just as if you're moving the cursor using the [Right Arrow] key.

3.7   Inserting and overstriking text

To add text, simply move the cursor to where you want the new text to appear, and type. You will normally be in the insert mode, and the text you type will be added to the existing text, which will be pushed to the right as you type.

The [Ins] key, however, is a toggle – each time you press it, you move from the insert mode to the overstrike mode, or vice versa. If you're in the overstrike mode, the characters you type will replace the characters already on the screen.

The cursor will change to show you which mode you are currently in. If you're inserting, the cursor will be just like the cursor you see in DOS, a blinking underscore character; if you're overstriking, the cursor will appear as a half block.

To illustrate the difference between inserting and overstriking, let's look at the following text, with the cursor positioned as shown:

```
response to your letter of Jan. 23
I would like to remind you of the legal
implications of such a move.
```

To change the date from Jan. 23 to Feb 10 in the insert mode, we would first type the new date:

```
response to your letter of Feb. 10Jan. 23
I would like to remind you of the legal
implications of such a move.
```

and then delete the old date:

```
response to your letter of Feb. 10_
I would like to remind you of the legal
implications of such a move.
```

In this case, overstriking would be more convenient because we wouldn't have to delete any characters:

```
response to your letter of Jan. 23
I would like to remind you of the legal
implications of such a move.
```

We can simply type the new date. As we type, the new characters will replace the characters beneath them and, when we finish, the screen will look like this:

```
response to your letter of Feb. 10
I would like to remind you of the legal
implications of such a move.
```

3.8   Marking blocks

A block of text is any group of characters on the screen. It can be one character, one word, one line, part of a paragraph, many pages — any amount of text, including the entire document. Several operations are called block operations because they involve marking a block so that *Norton Textra* can do something with it. These operations include *Highlight* (**4.5**), *Spell check*

(**4.7**), *Delete block* (**4.9**), *Copy block* (**5.6**), and *Move block* (**5.7**), as well as certain operations within *Print* and *Save*.

The cursor should be at the beginning or end of the block when you press the keys to begin the command. To mark the block you can use the cursor keys (**3.3.1**) or any of the shortcuts listed. The block you are marking will be highlighted as you mark it, so that you can see exactly what you have marked. When the block you want is marked, press [Enter]. The block operation you have chosen will be performed.

The shortcuts that you can use for marking blocks are listed to the right of the prompts:

```
L - Line
W - Word
S - Sentence
P - Paragraph
```

[L] will mark the line, or the remainder of the line, to the right of the cursor. [W] will mark the word, or the remainder of the word, to the right of the cursor. [S] will mark the sentence, or the remainder of the sentence, to the right of the cursor. [P] will mark the paragraph, or the remainder of the paragraph, to the right of the cursor.

You may also use the cursor keys and shortcuts in combination until the block you want is marked. Then press [Enter] and the block operation you have chosen will be performed.

4

Editing a Document

4.1   The *Edit* menu

The *Edit menu* looks like this:

```
F1 more...      F2 insert line  F3 new format   F4 highlight   F5  handbook
F6 spell check F7 delete line   F8 delete block  F9 delete word F10 undelete
```

4.2   More...   [F1]

[F1] cycles through *Norton Textra*'s three editing menus. The first of these menus is the one shown above. Pressing [F1] will cycle to the *Shift* menu (see **5.1**). Pressing [F1] again will cycle to the *Alt* menu (see **6.1**). And pressing [F1] once more will return you to the *Edit* menu. This menu cycle is described in more detail in **3.2.1**.

4.3   Insert line   [F2]

[F2] inserts a blank line in front of (above) the current line, and moves the cursor to the beginning of the blank line. This command is useful when you want to insert a good deal of new text in the middle of existing text, when it would be annoying (and confusing) to have to push a line of text in front of you while you typed in a new paragraph. For example:

```
Jupiter
Saturn
Neptune_
Pluto
```

You suddenly realize that you have left something out. Press [F2] and you will see this:

```
Jupiter
Saturn

Neptune
Pluto
```

Now you can type the missing name in the blank space created:

```
Jupiter
Saturn
Uranus_
Neptune
Pluto
```

4.4   New format   [F3]

[F3]/New format allows you to change margins and indents, line spacing, paragraph styles, and even type styles, within your document — whether for the whole document or for different parts of it. Seven formats are available automatically in *Norton Textra*, as shown in the *New format* menu:

```
F1 - Main document format
F2 - Indented quote
F3 - Single spacing
F4 - Centered lines
F5 - (unused)
F6 - Works cited format
F7 - Endnote format

F9 - Edit these formats
```

Note that [F9] gives you the opportunity to change any of these formats (you can also edit formats directly from the *Edit* menu by pressing [Alt F3]-see **6.4**).

To select a new format, press the function key corresponding to the format you want. You will return to the editor where a ruler for the new format has been inserted at the cursor position. (This ruler will show up on screen, but it will not print out when you print your document. You can, if you wish, tell *Norton Textra* not to display the markers for format changes — see **6.7.5**). All text you type in below the new ruler will be automatically formatted to its specifications.

You can return to the previous format or change to a new one by again pressing [F3]. You can remove a format change and ruler by using [Del] or [Backspace] to delete the format change marker. When you delete a format ruler, the text that had been formatted to its specifications will be automatically reformatted to the specifications of the previous ruler.

4.5   Highlight   [F4]

You can highlight your text **in bold**, underline it, or **do both**. *Norton Textra* can also take advantage of other features your printer might have, such as italics, compressed type, or different fonts.

The *[F4]/Highlight* command leads to a menu that will vary depending on what printer you have told *Norton Textra* you are working with (see **8.3.1**). The *Highlighting* menu for the Epson LX800, for example, looks like this:

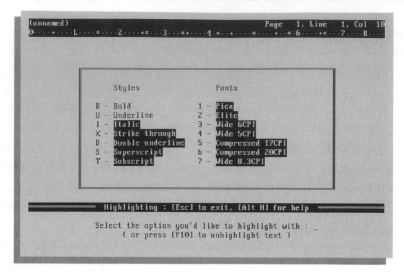

(CPI stands for characters per inch.)

Your printer may offer different options than these for highlighting text. For an especially important document like a résumé, you may want to get access to a versatile printer and make use of *Norton Textra*'s abilities to highlight your text.

At the bottom of the screen will be the prompt

```
Select the option or font you'd like to highlight with : _
          ( or press [F10] to unhighlight text )
```

4.5.1   Highlighting existing text

The *[F4]/Highlight* command lets you highlight any block of text in one of several different styles, such as bold or underline, or fonts, such as pica, compressed, or Helvetica. Text that is not highlighted is said to be in the normal font. Another way of saying this text is bold is to say this text is highlighted in bold.

After you have pressed [F4], the *highlighting* menu will appear and *Norton Textra* will prompt you to select one of the styles or fonts listed in the menu. After you have selected one, *Norton Textra* will prompt you to mark the block (see **3.8**) that you want highlighted.

As you move the cursor during this step, the text will be highlighted appropriately. If you selected the bold font, for example, the text will be highlighted in bold as you mark it.

When you've painted the text you want to highlight, press [Enter] again. You will be returned to the editor.

4.5.2   Highlighting text as you enter it

You can also highlight text as you enter it. When you reach a point in your typing when you want to highlight the material you enter, you can press either [Ctrl F] from the editor or [F] from the *Options* menu (**6.10**). You will see a menu like the *Highlight* menu, where you can choose any style or font supported by your current printer (**8.3.1**) by pressing the indicated letter or number. You will then return to the editor where you will see the text you add highlighted in the style or font you have selected.

When you wish to return to normal font (or switch to another), press either [Ctrl F] or [Alt F10], [F] again. Press the letter or number of the style or font you want, or press [F10] to return to normal.

4.5.3   Unhighlighting

Pressing [F10] from the *Highlighting* menu will allow you to return existing text to the normal font. After you have pressed [F10], *Norton Textra* will prompt you to:

> **Now move the cursor anywhere within the highlighted area, then press [Enter]..._**

Press [Enter], the block will be returned to normal, and you can begin editing again.

4.6   Handbook   [F5]

Pressing [F5] will give you instant help from the online handbook. You have important rules and suggestions about writing immediately available to you whenever and wherever you are working. You also have complete freedom of access to the contents of the handbook; unlike bound pages, the handbook screens are not linked in an unvarying sequence. Merely by choosing a keystroke (from choices always displayed on the screen), you will be able to move instantly from any one section of the handbook to another.

There are three different online handbooks that work with *Norton Textra*. The label on your original *Norton Textra* program disk will tell you if *The Confident Writer* or *Writing: A College Handbook* (**4.6.4**) is the handbook on your disk, as will the copyright screen that appears briefly when you load *Norton Textra*. If neither of these names appears then you are using the stand-alone version (**4.6.3**).

4.6.1 Using the online handbook

You can use *Norton Textra* quite successfully without ever using the online handbook. In fact, if you are actually *writing*–if your fingers are moving over the keyboard and your mind is succeeding in finding how to express something and what to say next–you should keep writing. Leave questions about paragraph structure, proper spelling or punctuation, or precise documentation of sources until the ideas dry up or your fingers get tired.

If you are having trouble discovering ideas, however, and find yourself watching the cursor blink, go to the handbook for a number of approaches to solving your problem. The handbook also offers help on other problems, such as finding and developing a thesis, ordering your ideas, crafting a beginning or ending, and so forth. When your work is in fairly good shape, the handbook's suggestions for revision can help you reshape and then polish it. Some of the suggestions may send you to other parts of the handbook for help.

In your revisions, you or a willing friend may, whether on screen or on paper, use the editing or correction symbols; or your instructor may use them in marking up your work. Use the menu of symbols in the online handbook to help you redevelop and revise your document as needed, always beginning with the largest changes and ending, when you are fairly well satisfied with your efforts, with the editorial changes of spelling, punctuation, and mechanics.

And, of course, any time that your writing process is slowed by a nagging concern about a question of grammar or punctuation, turn to the online handbook for help.

4.6.2 The handbook screens

All topic menus, sub-menus, and text screens of the online handbook derive from the original table of contents, which appears when you press [F5] from the *Edit* menu. You can press any of the options offered onscreen, or you can press [Home] if you want to return to the table of contents.

Lines 16–23 of your screen will provide a window containing the eight lines of your text surrounding the cursor at the time you pressed [F5] to access the handbook – thus enabling you to see the text containing your question while moving through the handbook looking for an answer.

When you find the part of the handbook with the help you are looking for, you can press [Alt F] to freeze the handbook on the screen. *Norton Textra* will return you to your document, where you can edit just as you normally would. When you want to remove the handbook from the screen, press [Alt U].

4.6.3 The stand-alone version

The stand-alone version of the online handbook has been prepared by Myron C. Tuman of the University of Alabama. It is a concise handbook of grammar and rhetoric, and you can use it by itself or in conjunction with any writing handbook.

Pressing [F5] from the *Edit* menu will bring up the *Handbook* menu:

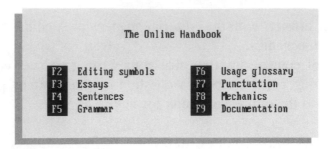

Pressing any of the indicated function keys will move you to one of the eight associated topic menus where another screen of choices will provide direct access to handbook information. Pressing [Esc] will return you directly to your document (as it will at any time inside the online handbook).

F2 - Editing symbols

This topic menu offers a simple means of gaining access to the handbook sections that are tied to common editing symbols. This screen will be of particular help to you when you are using *Norton Textra* to revise a draft that has been edited by your instructor or by a classmate – whether from a hand-written draft, from a print-out (hardcopy), or from the document file itself (editing online), in which case the symbols could be typed in using the *Comment* function (see **6.8**).

In any case, all you have to do is move the highlighted block to the desired correction symbol using the four cursor control arrows (→ ← ↓ ↑). As the highlighted block moves from symbol to symbol, a brief description of that symbol will appear in a box in the center of the screen with an accompanying prompt telling you to press [Enter] for more information.

F3 - Essays

This topic menu offers nine choices having to do with the writing process as a whole and the essay as rhetorical unit.

F4 - Sentences

This topic menu offers seventeen text screens.

F5 - Grammar

This topic menu offers ten selections, each of which leads to an associated sub-menu with additional choices.

F6 - Usage glossary

This topic menu offers 125 selections displayed on a series of six screens linked by [PgDn] and [PgUp]. To see any one of the initial twenty-five selections, merely press the indicated letter; to see any of the following five screens, merely use [PgDn] (or [PgUp]).

F7 - Punctuation

This topic menu offers twelve selections, a number of which have their own sub-menus.

F8 - Mechanics

This topic menu offers twelve choices dealing with three large areas: the overall layout of a college essay, special problems relating to computer-prepared documents, and traditional questions concerning capital letters, titles, abbreviations, underlining, and numbers.

F9 - Documentation

This topic menu offers advice on how and what to document in academic writing. Examples of specific citations are given in the *Endnote* (**6.9**) and *Works cited* (**6.5**) commands.

4.6.4 The three other online handbooks

Norton Textra is also available in three additional versions, each with a different online handbook keyed to a specific W. W. Norton textbook.

Here is the opening screen of the online handbook based on the second edition of *The Confident Writer: A Norton Handbook* by Constance J. Gefvert.

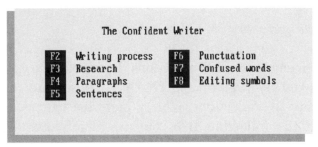

Here is the opening screen of the online handbook based on the third edition of *Writing: A College Handbook* by James A. W. Heffernan and John Lincoln.

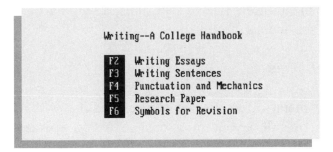

Here is the opening screen of the online handbook based on *The Norton Guide to Writing* by Thomas Cooley:

Each of these handbooks works in the same way. Press the indicated function key or letter to move to the desired screen; the [Home] key to move back to the next menu; the [PgUp] and [PgDn] keys to move through the handbook one screen at a time; [Alt F] to freeze any screen while you edit; and [Esc] to remove the handbook screens and return to your document.

4.7   Spell check   [F6]

Spell check offers you an online dictionary that enables you to check the spelling of all or part of your document and to look up one word at a time or browse through the entire contents of the dictionary.

There are four main keystrokes to remember:

- [F6] calls up the *Spell check* menu (see below).

- [Ctrl K] allows you to spell check the remainder of your document (from the current cursor position to the end of the document) without going through the *Spell check* menu.

- [Ctrl L] looks up the spelling of the current word.

- [Ctrl B] lets you browse in the dictionary. *Norton Textra* will display the first nine words beginning with the letter or letters you have typed at the prompt. When you find the word you want, press the number key indicated to its left; the word will be inserted at the current cursor position.

4.7.1   The Spell check menu

Pressing [F6] from the *Edit* menu brings up the *Spell check* menu:

```
    Spell checking features

S - Spell check the current document
P - Spell check a portion of the current document


    Spell checking options

A - Automatically suggest corrections      - Off
D - Check for doubled words (e.g.,  the the) - On
N - Check for non-words       (e.g.,  RM412)  - Off
O - Check for one character words (e.g.,  B) - Off
R - Allow automatic word replacement        - On

H - Display hyphens when browsing           - On




============ Spell check : [Esc] to exit, [Alt H] for help ============
                    Select command : _
```

4.7.2   Spell checking features

S - Spell check the current document

When you press [S], *Norton Textra* will begin checking. In the
lower left of the screen you will be told **Spell check is
XX% complete**. This message indicates how much of the
document *Norton Textra* has checked. In the lower right you will
be told that you can **Press [Esc] to quit spell
checking**.

When *Norton Textra* finds a spelling error (that is, a word not
in its dictionary), you will hear a distinctive beep. The following
menu will be displayed:

```
Word not found : Benjy

S - Suggest some corrections
R - Remember this word (it's O.K.)
I - Ignore this word
M - Manually correct
```

[S]/Suggest some corrections searches the dictionary for
Norton Textra's best guesses for the word you meant to type.
Any guesses will be listed, each with a letter next to it. You can
select a suggestion by pressing the appropriate letter or you can

press [Esc] to cancel these suggestions and return to the previous menu.

[R]/Remember this word (it's O.K.) tells *Norton Textra* that the word is correct as typed and that you want *Norton Textra* to remember it.

[I]/Ignore this word tells *Norton Textra* to ignore the word for the remainder of the document. It won't be saved permanently when you return to DOS after finishing with *Norton Textra*.

[M]/Manually correct brings up the prompt **Enter correction**. Type in the correction you want to make and press [Enter]. *Norton Textra* will make the correction both here and anywhere else the misspelled word is found.

If the [R] option is not offered in the menu, it means that there is no more room for *Norton Textra* to remember words, which can happen right away in machines with very small memories (256K) or in large-memory machines when the supplemental dictionary grows full. When this happens, you can use the *Compress* program (**4.7.4**) to add some of your personal words into the main dictionary, thereby freeing up room for more words in WORDS.LST.

Norton Textra's dictionary contains upper and lower case information, so the spell checker will stop on words that are incorrectly capitalized, such as *california*. *Norton Textra* will alert you to this by using the message **Case mismatch** instead of **Word not found**.

P - Spell check a portion of the current document

After pressing [P], you will be prompted to mark the portion of the document that you want checked. Spell check will then proceed as above.

4.7.3   Spell checking options

A - Automatically suggest corrections

If this switch is on, *Norton Textra* will automatically suggest a list of corrections whenever it finds a misspelled word. If it is off, a menu will appear as described above.

D - Check for doubled words (e.g., the the)

If this switch is on, *Norton Textra* will stop if it finds the same word twice in a row in your document. You will be prompted:

> **Doubled word was found**
>
> **D - Delete the extra word**
> **O - It's O.K., continue checking**

N - Check for non-words (e.g., RM412)

This switch controls whether *Norton Textra* stops on non-words while spell checking your document. A non-word is any word that contains both alphabetic and non-alphabetic characters, such as RM412, or R2D2.

O - Check for one character words (e.g., B)

This switch controls whether *Norton Textra* spell checks one-character words. If it's off, *Norton Textra* will ignore all words of a single character.

R - Allow automatic word replacement

To save you the time of telling *Norton Textra* what you meant to type in cases where a typo or misspelling is obvious, *Norton Textra*'s dictionary contains about 125 automatic replacements that will be made if this switch is on.

absense	(=absence)	heighth	(=height)
accesible	(=accessible)	hinderance	(=hindrance)
accomodate	(=accommodate)	hypocrasy	(=hypocrisy)
accomodations	(=accommodations)	imediately	(=immediately)
accompaning	(=accompanying)	independant	(=independent)
acheivement	(=achievement)	indispensible	(=indispensable)
acknowlege	(=acknowledge)	insistance	(=insistence)
acknowlegment	(=acknowledgment)	instalation	(=installation)
acurate	(=accurate)	intelectual	(=intellectual)
acuse	(=accuse)	inteligent	(=intelligent)
acustomed	(=accustomed)	interferance	(=interference)
adolesent	(=adolescent)	interuption	(=interruption)
adress	(=address)	intolerence	(=intolerance)
aggresive	(=aggressive)	irelevant	(=irrelevant)
agravate	(=aggravate)	irresistable	(=irresistible)
ajacent	(=adjacent)	knowlege	(=knowledge)
allmost	(=almost)	maintainance	(=maintenance)
allready	(=already)	miscelaneous	(=miscellaneous)
appearence	(=appearance)	mispell	(=misspell)
arguement	(=argument)	narative	(=narrative)
attendence	(=attendance)	neccessary	(=necessary)
begining	(=beginning)	nieghbor	(=neighbor)
catagory	(=category)	niether	(=neither)
comercial	(=commercial)	nineth	(=ninth)
comission	(=commission)	ninty	(=ninety)
competance	(=competence)	oticable	(=noticeable)
conceed	(=concede)	ocasion	(=occasion)
concievable	(=conceivable)	occurence	(=occurrence)
concieve	(=conceive)	occurrance	(=occurrence)
congradulation	(=congratulation)	ocurring	(=occurring)
congradulations	(=congratulations)	omision	(=omission)
correspondance	(=correspondence)	ommission	(=omission)
decieve	(=deceive)	oparate	(=operate)
dilema	(=dilemma)	oparation	(=operation)
disasterous	(=disastrous)	oportunities	(=opportunities)
enterance	(=entrance)	overwelming	(=overwhelming)
entrepraneur	(=entrepreneur)	paralell	(=parallel)
equiped	(=equipped)	paralize	(=paralyze)
exagerate	(=exaggerate)	parallell	(=parallel)
exagerating	(=exaggerating)	pasttime	(=pastime)
excede	(=exceed)	peacable	(=peaceable)
excelent	(=excellent)	peice	(=piece)
existance	(=existence)	percieve	(=perceive)
extravegant	(=extravagant)	permisible	(=permissible)
favorate	(=favorite)	perseverence	(=perseverance)
feasable	(=feasible)	persistant	(=persistent)
foriegn	(=foreign)	plausable	(=plausible)
forteen	(=fourteen)	posession	(=possession)
fourty	(=forty)	predominent	(=predominant)
freind	(=friend)	preferance	(=preference)

prefered	(=preferred)	seperate	(=separate)
preperation	(=preparation)	sheperd	(=shepherd)
priviledge	(=privilege)	significance	(=significance)
procede	(=proceed)	sincerly	(=sincerely)
prominant	(=prominent)	succesful	(=successful)
propriator	(=proprietor)	supercede	(=supersede)
questionaire	(=questionnaire)	teh	(=the)
reciept	(=receipt)	tommorow	(=tomorrow)
recievable	(=receivable)	tommorrow	(=tomorrow)
recieve	(=receive)	transfered	(=transferred)
referance	(=reference)	truely	(=truly)
regretable	(=regrettable)	wierd	(=weird)
rememberance	(=remembrance)	yeild	(=yield)

4.7.4   The Compress utility program

For any one of a number of reasons you may eventually have a need to modify *Norton Textra*'s compressed dictionary. For instance, after using the spell checker for a long time you may accumulate a large supplemental dictionary, decreasing the performance of the spell checker. You can alleviate this by merging the file WORDS.LST into *Norton Textra*'s main dictionary and starting a new supplemental dictionary. COMPRESS.EXE allows you to do this.

You will need the compress program (COMPRESS.EXE) and the file of raw words that you intend to compress. If you are merging words into an existing dictionary, you will also need a copy of that dictionary. In addition, if you have a floppy-based system, you will need a disk for the new dictionary. Make sure this disk has enough room to accommodate your new dictionary (at least 200,000 bytes for a new main dictionary).

Format of the raw word file

The raw word file should be a pure ASCII file (**9.3.1**) with one word on each line. Each word can be optionally followed by at least one space and a group of operators (see below). These operators must be surrounded by parentheses and separated by commas.

Hyphenation is produced by typing a period at the position where the hyphen occurs (e.g., pe.ri.od).

The acceptable cases of a word are determined by the case in which the word appears plus the cases specified by a set of case operators (see examples below).

Apostrophes (for contractions such as *can't*) and hard hyphens (for compound words such as *cross-examine*) can be embedded directly.

Since periods are used for indicating hyphenation, a colon is used for denoting abbreviations such as A.M. See the example below.

These are the valid operators that can follow a word:

OPERATOR	MEANING
ALLcaps	Word is valid in all capital letters (*NASA*).
PROper	Word is valid as proper noun (*Textra*).
LOWercase	Word is valid in lower case (*computer*).
DELete	Delete this word from dictionary.
=XXXX	The word *XXXX* is to be automatically substituted for the word on the left of the equals sign. This operator must be the last one on the line since the string is terminated by ")", and can be used to automatically correct misspellings.

These examples illustrate these operators:

RAW WORD	MEANING
Bill (lowercase)	*Bill* and *bill* are acceptable.
NASA	*NASA* is only correct form.
PASCAL (proper)	*PASCAL* and *Pascal* are acceptable.
acheive (=achieve)	Substitute *achieve* when *acheive* appears.
proc.es.sor	Syllables are divided after the *c* and after the first *s*.
a-ok (allcaps)	*A-OK* and *a-ok* are acceptable.
A:M:	Abbreviation for *A.M.*
would've	A new contraction.
Wordstar (DEL)	Eliminate the word *Wordstar* from the dictionary.

Starting Compress

To start the program, insert the program disk, type COMPRESS
and then press [Enter]. The following menu will appear:

```
F1 - Exit to DOS
F2 - Sort a list of words
F5 - Add words to main dictionary
     (MAIN.WRD)
```

[F2]/Sorting the raw word file

Press [F2] to sort the raw word file. You will be prompted for
the name of the file you want to sort. (If you just press [Enter],
Norton Textra will assume you want to sort WORDS.LST). Enter
the name of your file, including a full path specification if
necessary (e.g., CUSTOM.SRT or C:\TEXTRA\WORDS.LST).

The sorted words will be saved in a file called WORDS.SRT. If there is already a document on your disk with that name, you will be prompted for a new filename.

Prompts will inform you of the progress of the sorting (e.g., reading, sorting, writing). When sorting is completed, you will return to the *Compress* menu.

[F5]/Adding words to the dictionary

Once the file is sorted, press [F5] to add it to the main dictionary. You will be prompted to enter the name of the file that contains the words you want to add (WORDS.SRT is assumed). Once you've specified a filename, *Compress* will take the following steps:

1. If the dictionary you're adding words to doesn't exist, you will be asked if you want to create a new dictionary (this allows you to create specialized dictionaries).

2. If it does exist, a backup will be made and renamed (MAIN.WRD will become OLDMAIN.WRD).

3. *Compress* will add the words contained in the file you're merging from, creating a new file in the process (MAIN.WRD).

If errors are found in the raw word file, a boxed window will report the erroneous word and the type of error that occurred. When this happens, make a list of the errors, correct the errors in the raw word file, and compress it again.

Common errors include embedding illegal characters in raw words or having words out of order (because you did not sort the raw word file first).

Keep a copy of each list of words you add, so that you can reconstruct your personalized dictionaries if your current MAIN.WRD gets damaged somehow.

Using Compress on floppy disk systems

To add words to a main dictionary on a dual floppy system, use the following steps:

1. In the A: disk drive, put a disk that contains the words you're going to add (e.g., WORDS.LST), and a copy of the *Compress* program (COMPRESS.EXE).

2. Place the disk that contains a copy of the main dictionary (MAIN.WRD) in the B: disk drive.

3. From the A: disk drive, start the *Compress* program. When *Compress* doesn't find MAIN.WRD on the A: disk drive, it will ask you:

```
Main.wrd does not exist.
Create a new Main.wrd (Y/N): _
```

Press [N] for no. *Compress* will then ask you to **Enter dictionary name**. Now type B:MAIN.WRD. *Compress* will now read the original words from B:, and create the new dictionary file on A:.

4.8   Delete line   [F7]

[F7] deletes the current line. It doesn't matter where the cursor is positioned when you press [F7] – the entire line will be deleted. For example:

```
The ease with which you can manipulate
text, moving words, sentences,
paragraphs, and more, is one of the
great advantages of word processing.
```

Pressing [F7] once will yield

```
The ease with which you can manipulate
text, moving words, sentences, great
advantages of word processing.
```

If you've made a mistake, press [F10] to undelete (see **4.11**).

4.9   Delete block   [F8]

[F8] allows you to mark a block of text to be deleted. (See **3.8** on marking blocks.)

    The text will be highlighted on the screen as you mark it, so it will always be clear just what you're marking. As soon as you've pressed [Enter] the marked block will be deleted.

    If you've made a mistake, press [F10] to undelete (see **4.11**).

4.10   Delete word   [F9]

[F9] deletes the word to the right of the cursor. If the cursor is positioned at the beginning of a word, the entire word will be deleted. If the cursor is positioned in the middle of the word, the end of the word will be deleted.

    If you've made a mistake, press [F10] to undelete (see **4.11**).

4.11 Undelete   [F10]

[F10] will recover deleted text. Whenever you delete, the message **Press [F10] to "undelete"** appears at the top of the screen. This is a visual clue that text has been deleted, in case you accidentally press a key and aren't sure just what you've done. More important, it reminds you that you can recover the deleted text.

    All text deleted since the appearance of this message can be recovered by pressing [F10]. The message will remain until you press any key other than a delete key. When you do this, the deletions become permanent, and the text cannot be recovered. Note: Unless the material has been previously saved. If you find that you have mistakenly deleted important material and can no longer undelete it, save and exit the current file, and retrieve the automatic backup file (*Norton Textra* will have used your filename plus the extension BAK). If the material you want is still there, save the file with a new name **(9.7)** – you cannot save a file with the BAK extension.

5

Editing a document

5.1 The *Shift* menu

```
F1 more...    F2 split screen F3 search  F4 replace     F5 copy block
F6 move block F7 print    F8 page layout  F9 merge/browse F10 save options
```

[F7]/Print will be discussed in chapter 8; *[F8]/Page layout* will be discussed in chapter 7; *[F10]/Save options* will be discussed in chapter 9.

You don't need to call up this menu in order to begin these commands. Instead, from the *Edit* menu you can press [Shift] along with the appropriate function key on the *Shift* menu. [Shift F3], for example, begins the *Search* command.

5.2 More...   [F1]

[F1] cycles through *Norton Textra*'s three editing menus (see **3.2.1**). Pressing [F1] from the *Shift* menu will cycle to the *Alt* menu (see **6.1**). Pressing [F1] once more will return you to the *Edit* menu (see **4.1**).

5.3 Split screen   [Shift F2]

The *Split screen* command enables you to look at more than one part of your document at a time, or to look at more than one document at a time, or both. You can split the screen into as many as eight windows at once, with each of the windows being the size you want.

You might, for example, want to keep the introductory paragraph to a paper onscreen as you draft or revise the conclusion. You might want to keep a file of notes onscreen as you draft a document. You might want to keep your résumé onscreen as you draft a letter of application. Split screen makes it easy to see two or more pieces of text at once and also to move or copy blocks between them.

Clearly, once you have more than two or three windows onscreen at once, at least some of the windows are going to be too small to show you significant amounts of text. Nevertheless, these windows may serve as convenient place markers in files that you need to go back to frequently in your work session. Like a desk covered with notebooks, note cards, and books (open or filled with bookmarks) that you keep turning to as you write, your screen may have one big window for the document you are hard at work on, as well as several little windows like bookmarks for things you may need to look up from time to time.

5.3.1   The Split screen menu

When you start the *Split screen* command, you will be offered the following choices:

```
H - Split horizontal
V - Split vertical
C - Close window
Z - Zoom window  Ctrl Z
N - Next window   Ctrl N
```

At the bottom of the screen you will be prompted to **Select command**.

5.3.2   H - Horizontal split, V - Vertical split

[H] and [V] enable you to split the screen from side to side or from top to bottom. Once you have pressed either key, a horizontal or vertical line will appear in the middle of the screen (or in the middle of the active window). You will be prompted to move this line up or down if it is horizontal, or left or right if it is vertical, by using the arrow keys; move the line until it splits the screen as you wish and then press [Enter].

5.3.3   Choosing a document for the new window

Once you have placed the line splitting the screen, you will be prompted to choose whether you want to

> **Use same document, create a document, or**
> **retrieve a document ([S]/[C]/[R]) : _**

Use same document

If you press [S], you will be returned to the editor with two pieces of the current document onscreen. The cursor will be in the new window.

Create a document

If you press [C], you will return to the editor with the current document and a new blank document onscreen. The cursor will be in the new document.

Retrieve a document

If you press [R], you will be taken to a menu like the *Retrieve document* menu (**2.5.1**), where you can choose a document in the current directory or one from a different directory or disk. Once you have chosen a document, press [Enter]. You will be returned to the editor with the current document and the newly retrieved document both onscreen. The cursor will be in the newly retrieved document.

5.3.4   The current or active window

The *current* or *active* window is the one where the cursor is; it is the window where you can perform all the normal editing functions. *Norton Textra* will indicate the active window by a formatting ruler: the ruler will appear at the top of the active window and the cursor will appear somewhere within that window.

Z - Zoom window Ctrl Z

[Z] is a toggle that allows you to enlarge a window up to full size, or to return it to smaller size so that the other open windows will show. If you have created a small window simply to keep a document at hand as you work, you may suddenly need to read something in it or look something up; *zooming* the window enables you to do this.

You can also zoom the current window up or down from the editor by pressing [Ctrl Z].

C - Close window

[C] allows you to close the current window. If this window is the only open window for that particular document and if you have made changes to the document, *Norton Textra* will ask

```
Changes have been made to this document,
but not saved to disk.

Do you want to save it first _
     ([Y] or [N], [Esc] to cancel) ?
```

Press [Esc] if you change your mind and want either to choose another option or to continue editing this document, leaving the window open. Press [Y] if you want to save the current work before closing the window. Press [N] if you don't want to save the changes. If you press [Y] or [N], *Norton Textra* will transfer you to the next window.

If no windows are open—only your original document—you will hear an error beep.

N - Switch to next window

[N] allows you to leave the current window and make the next window the active one. Next in this context refers to the order in which you created the windows. If you have several windows open, you may need to press [N] several times before you reach the window you want.

You can also switch to the next window from the editor by pressing [Ctrl N].

5.4   Search   [Shift F3]

When your documents are small, you can easily find your way around them by paging up and down with the [PgUp] and [PgDn] key. But as your documents grow larger, it's not so easy. The *Search* command can be used to locate an area of your document quickly by looking for a word or phrase that you know is located there.

5.4.1   The *Search* menu

When you start the *Search* command, the following menu will appear:

```
Enter search string : _

F5 confirm   F6 ignore case   F8 forward   F9 any string
```

At this point you can type in the string you want to search for, or press any of the specified keys [F5]−[F9]. The string can be any group of up to forty characters−"string," or "Textra," or "October 15, 1988." Or it could be "str", or "xtr", or "15", −you just want to give enough so that the string will occur only once in the file and *Norton Textra* can get you there quickly.

Keys [F5], [F6], [F8], and [F9] are *toggles* that govern how the *Search* command works−each time you press one of these keys, the option will change value, as discussed below. You can turn switches on or off any time before pressing the [Enter] key to begin the search. When you start the *Search* command, the switches will have the same value they had at the end of the last *Search* command.

5.4.2   F5 *confirm*, F5 *no confirm*

The *confirm* option is useful in searching for one instance of a string that appears many times within the text. If *no confirm* is on, the first match found will be used; if *confirm* is on, you will be asked each time a match is found if this is the one you want. The message

O.K. ([Y] or [N]) ?

will appear. The cursor will be positioned underneath the first character of the matching string.

If you press [Y], the search will end, and you'll return to the editor. If you press [N], *Norton Textra* will continue searching.

5.4.3   F6 *ignore case*, F6 *match case*

If *ignore case* is on, matches to the search string will be found if the letters match, even if one is upper case and one is lower case. The search string *sample*, for example, would match any of the follow strings:

sample   SAMPLE   Sample   SaMpLe

If the match case switch is on, the case must match exactly: *Sample* would not be offered as a match for *sample*.

5.4.4   F8 *forward*, F8 *backward*

This switch controls which direction *Norton Textra* will search for the target string. *Norton Textra* begins searching at the current cursor position and moves either forward (toward the end of the file) or backward (toward the beginning), depending on how this switch is set.

5.4.5   F9 *whole words only,* F9 *any string*

For the search string "book", *any string* would find not only the word "book", but also "books", "bookkeeper", "handbook", and so forth. Whole words only would find only instances of the word "book."

5.4.6   Searching for the same string again

If you want to search again for the same string used in the last *Search* command, you can press [Ctrl S] from the editor. If no search string has been previously defined, you will hear a beep and remain in the editor.

5.5   Replace   [Shift F4]

Closely related to the *Search* command is the *Replace* command, which allows you to search for a string and replace it with any other string.

5.5.1 The *Replace* menu

When you start the *Replace* command, the following menu will appear:

```
Enter search string : _

F3 replace all F5 confirm F6 ignore case F8 forward F9 any string
```

At this point you can type in the string you want to search for, or press any of the specified keys [F3]–[F9]. The string can be any group of up to forty characters–"string", or "Textra", or "October 15, 1992." Or it could be "str", or "xtr", or "15",–you just want to give enough so that the string will occur only once in the file and *Norton Textra* can get you there quickly.

Press [Enter] when you're done entering the search string. You'll then be prompted to

Enter replacement : _

The same rules apply to the replacement string as for the search string, except that it can be up to 120 character long. After typing the replacement string, press [Enter] to begin. The search for the target string will begin at the current cursor position, and continue until either a match is found, or there is no more text to search. Note: it is possible that if the replacement string is longer than the search string, the message

This document is full. You must delete some text before adding more.

will appear. You must first delete some text before continuing with the *Replace* command.

If a match is found, one of the following will occur, depending on the setting of the *[F3]/replace all* and *[F5]/confirm* options (see **5.5.23**):

1. If *[F5]/confirm* is on, you will be asked whether you wish to replace this occurrence of the target string. If *[F3]/replace once* is also on, you will be returned to the editor after the first replacement you say yes to. If *[F3]/replace all* is on, you will be moved to the next occurrence of the target string and asked whether you wish to replace it.

2. If *[F5]/no confirm* and *[F3]/replace once* are on, this occurrence of the target string will be replaced with the replacement string, and you will return to the editor.

3. If *[F5]/no confirm* and *[F3]/replace all* are on, all occurrences of the target string will be replaced, and you will be returned to the editor.

If the search string is not found, the message **Not found!** is displayed, and a beep is heard. You will remain in the *Replace* command and may either try again or cancel the command and return to the editor.

Keys [F3], [F5], [F6], [F8], and [F9] are toggles that govern how the *Replace* command works—each time you press one of these keys, the option will change value, as discussed below. You can turn switches on or off any time before pressing the [Enter] key to begin the search. When you start the *Replace* command, the switches will have the same value they had at the end of the last *Replace* command.

5.5.2   F3 *replace all*, F3 *replace once*

If *replace all* is on, all occurrences of the target string will be replaced with the replacement string. If *[F5]/confirm* is also on, you will be queried (see **5.5.3**) before each replacement.

If *replace once* is on, only the first occurrence of the search string will be replaced.

5.5.3   F5 *confirm*, F5 *no confirm*

If *confirm* is on, you will be asked when a match is found if you wish to replace this particular occurrence of the search string with the replacement string. The message

$$\text{O.K. ([Y] or [N]) ?}$$

will appear. The cursor will be positioned underneath the first character of the matching string.

If you press [Y], the target string will be replaced with the replacement string. If you press [N], no replacement will be made, and *Norton Textra* will search for the next occurrence of the search string.

If *no confirm* is on, replacements will be made without confirmation.

5.5.4   F6 *ignore case*, F6 *match case*

If ignore case is on, matches to the search string will be found if the letters match, even if one is upper case and one is lower case. For example, the search string *sample* would match any of the following strings:

> sample   SAMPLE   Sample   SaMpLe

If match case is on, the case must match exactly: *Sample* would not be offered as a match for *sample*.

5.5.5   F8 *forward*, F8 *backward*

This switch controls which direction *Norton Textra* will search for the target string. *Norton Textra* begins searching at the current cursor position and moves either forward (toward the end of the file) or backward (toward the beginning), depending on how this switch is set.

5.5.6   F9 *whole words only*, F9 *any string*

For the search string *book*, *any string* would find not only the word "book", but also "books", "bookkeeper", "handbook", and so forth. Whole words only would find only instances of the word "book."

5.5.7   Replacing the same string again

If you want to search again for the same string used in the last *Search* or *Replace* command, you can press [Ctrl S] from the editor. If no search string has been previously defined, you will hear a beep and remain in the editor.

And if you want to replace a search string with the same replacement string used in the last *Replace* command, you can press [Ctrl R].

5.6   Copy block   [Shift F5]

The *Copy block* command is used to copy a block of text from one spot to another. The original block of text will remain where it was, and a copy of that block can be placed anywhere in your document.

When you start the *Copy block* command, you will be prompted to

> **Mark the text you want to copy,**
> **then press [Enter]...**

See **3.8** for instructions on marking blocks.

When you've marked the block of text you want to copy, press [Enter]. You will then be prompted to:

> **Now move cursor to the insertion spot,**
> **then press [Enter]...**

Move the cursor to the spot where you want to place the copy, and press [Enter]. The copy will be inserted in front of (to the left of) the spot you mark. After the copy has been made, you will return to the editor.

The insertion spot cannot be located within the marked block, with the exception of the first or last character of the block (this allows you to place the copy immediately above or below the original).

You can change your mind at any time, and cancel the *Copy block* command by pressing the [Esc] key.

You can copy the same block again by pressing [Ctrl C]. You will be prompted to move to the insertion spot.

5.7   Move block   [Shift F6]

The *Move block* command is used to move a block of text from one spot to another. It is very similar to the *Copy block* command (see **5.6**). When you start the *Move block* command, you will be prompted to

```
Mark the text you want to move,
then press [Enter]...
```

See **3.8** for instructions on marking blocks.

When you've marked the block of text you want to move, press [Enter]. You will then be prompted to:

```
Now move cursor to the insertion spot,
then press [Enter]...
```

Move the cursor to the spot where you want to place the block, and press [Enter]. The block will be inserted in front of (to the left of) the spot you mark. After the move has been made, you will return to the editor.

5.8   Merge/browse   [Shift F9]

The *Merge/browse* command can be used both to copy text from another file into the current document and to browse through another document without copying anything. In contrast to the *Split screen* command (**5.3**), the screen will show only one document at a time and you cannot edit the file you are merging from. On the other hand, there may be cases in which the *Split screen* command would require more memory than is available in order to load the documents you want; you may still be able to use the *Merge/browse* command.

When you start the *Merge/browse* command, the prompt

```
Now move the cursor to the insertion
spot,
then press [Enter]...
```

will appear. Position the cursor where you want to merge text and press [Enter]. If you're just going to browse in the second document, you don't have to position the cursor in any specific spot – just press [Enter]. *Norton Textra* will display the *Retrieve document* menu (**2.5.2**). From here, you can select the document you want to merge from or browse within.

After selecting a document (by typing in its name or number), *Norton Textra* will read it in, and display it on the screen. The prompt at the bottom of the screen will read:

> **Now move the cursor to the first**
> **character, then press [Enter] ...**

You can now move around in the second document. To browse, don't press [Enter] — just move around using the cursor keys. To stop browsing and return to the original document, press [Esc] twice.

If you press enter, you will be prompted

> **Mark the text you want to merge,**
> **then press [Enter] ...**

Use the cursor keys or the shortcuts listed on the screen to mark the text you want to merge. When you press enter, *Norton Textra* will return you to the edit screen of the original document. Your cursor will be located on the first letter of the newly merged text.

Note: When you press [Enter] after choosing the insertion spot, *Norton Textra* saves a temporary copy of the current document to disk. There must be enough room on the disk to copy the current document or the *Merge/browse* command won't work. If there isn't enough room, you will get an error message and be returned to the editor.

Also, you can switch disks before starting the *Merge/browse* command by replacing the disk containing original file with the new disk. Be sure to replace the original disk after completing the *Merge/browse* option.

If you try to mark a block of lines that would make the document too big to fit in the memory available, the message

> **The block you've marked is too big to be copied**

will appear.

6

Editing a Document

6.1 The *Alt* Menu

```
F1 more...    F2 high ASCII F3 edit formats F4 works cited F5  DOS access
F6 customize F7 comments    F8 statistics   F9 endnotes     F10 options
```

You don't need to call up this menu in order to begin these commands. Instead, from the *Edit* menu you can press [Alt] along with the appropriate function key on the *Alt* menu. [Alt F2], for example, begins the *High ASCII* command.

6.2   More...   [F1]

[F1] cycles through *Norton Textra*'s three editing menus (see **3.2.1**). Pressing [F1] from the *Alt* menu will return you to the *Edit* menu (see **4.1**).

6.3   High ASCII   [Alt F2]

High ASCII is a bit of computer jargon that is the quickest way to refer to the extended character set—characters in addition to numerals and the normal English alphabet. Such characters include foreign language characters (such as é and ñ), math characters ($\approx$, $\sqrt{\ }$), and certain graphics characters (⸬, ⊣‖). *Norton Textra* makes it easy to add these characters to your text in either of two ways:

1. While editing, hold down [Alt] while pressing a three numeral sequence on the numeric keypad. You can find the appropriate sequence in any chart of high ASCII characters; your printer manual probably contains such a

chart. For example, to use é press [Alt 130]; to use ≈ press [Alt 247]; to use ┤ press [Alt 182].

2. An easier way is to press [F2] from the *Alt* menu to reach the *High ASCII* menu. This menu shows you the possibilities onscreen. You can use the arrow keys to reach your selection and then press [Enter]. You will return to the editor with your selection in place.

The *High ASCII* menu looks like this:

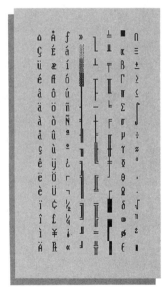

Not all printers will print all of these characters, so you may want to test the characters you want by printing out a draft before you spend a lot of time entering them throughout a document.

6.4   Edit formats   [Alt F3]

6.4.1   The *Edit formats* menu

The *Edit formats* command allows you to make changes in the seven formats or rulers that *Norton Textra* provides. When you press [F3] from the *Alt* menu (or select *[F9]/Edit these formats* on the *New format* menu – **4.4**), you will see the *Edit formats* menu:

```
      Main document format                    Current formats

L - Left margin        - 1.00"         F1 - Main document format
R - Right margin       - 1.00"         F2 - Indented quote
P - Paragraph indent   - 0.00"         F3 - Single spacing
                                       F4 - Centered lines
F - Default font       - Pica          F5 - (unused)
Y - Paragraph style    - Normal        F6 - Works cited format
S - Line spacing       - Double        F7 - Endnote format

M - Modify/set tabs
N - Change name of current format         Sample paragraph

                                          _____
                                          _____
                                          _____
                                          _____


        Edit formats : [Esc] to exit, [Alt H] for help

                   Select command : _
```

This menu in most ways overlaps the *Page layout* menu (**7.1**), where these options will be discussed.

The difference here, however, is that you can edit any of the seven formats so that they suit the particular document you are working on.

6.5   Works cited   [Alt F4]

Works cited greatly simplifies the task of giving documentary information for any sources you have cited within a paper. Advice is given within the *Online handbook* (**4.6.3**) for what to cite and how to cite it in a paper; this command helps you prepare the alphabetical list of citations that appears at the end of a documented paper. You will enter the necessary information, following the appropriate model given onscreen; *Norton Textra* will format the information with the proper indent for either MLA (Modern Language Association) or APA (American Psychological Association) style and alphabetize the citations for you.

When you begin the *Works cited* command, you will be taken to a screen headed **List of works cited**. If no entries have yet been made for the document, you will be told **No works cited yet....** If entries have already been made, you will be shown the first ones and the message **[PgUp], [PgDn] for more...**

At the bottom of the screen you will be offered the options

```
A   add a new work to the list    D   delete a work
M   modify a work   G generate works cited   P print works cited
```

If you press [A] to add a new work, you will be taken to a new screen with these instructions:

```
Type in the reference, press [Esc] when you're finished
Press [F5] to see examples of other common formats
Current documentation format is MLA (press [Alt F1] for APA)
```

Below these instructions appears a sample work cited entry for a book with one author, the format you will probably need most often. If, however, the source you want to cite is of another kind, press [F5] to cycle through other samples. The samples will be offered in MLA or APA format; [Alt F1] toggles between the two. Your instructor will tell you whether one is to be preferred for the paper you are writing; in general, MLA style works well for papers in English and the other humanities, and APA for papers in the social and natural sciences.

Type the reference in, following the sample for spacing, punctuation, capitalization, and specific information. Press [Esc] when you have finished. *Norton Textra* will keep your works cited entries properly formatted and alphabetized. When you print your document, you can print just the document itself or the document plus the list of works cited (**8.4.2**).

6.6   DOS access   [Alt F5]

The *DOS access* command allows you to execute DOS commands such as FORMAT, COPY, or CHKDSK while within *Norton Textra* (see appendix B for more about DOS). You can also run other programs from within *Norton Textra* and then return to *Norton Textra*, just as if you never left.

When you start the command, the *DOS access* menu will appear. The top portion of the screen lists *Pre-defined DOS commands*; the bottom portion of the screen contains a "pseudo-DOS prompt," where you can type in any DOS command, just as if you were at the real DOS prompt. You can also select any of the options listed at the top of the screen or define further ones.

6.6.1 Pre-defined DOS commands

Use [F1]−[F5]to set up the DOS commands you frequently use. You can then start each one with a single keystroke.

[F1] has been assigned the DOS command `DIR A:`. If you press [F1], *Norton Textra* will temporarily return control to DOS, the A: disk drive will spin, and DOS will list the files on that disk. The prompt `Press [Esc] to return to Textra` will appear. Pressing any key will return you to the *DOS access* menu where you can press [Esc] to return to your document or choose another DOS option.

To set a pre-defined DOS command, press any unoccupied key [F1]−[F5]. You will be prompted to

        `Enter new DOS command : _`

        `(press [F10] to insert the name`
                        `of the current document)`

Type in the command you want to assign to this key.

The [F10] option allows you to set up pre-defined DOS commands that work with the current document. For example, if you are using *Norton Textra* on a hard disk but like occasionally to make a copy of the current document onto a floppy disk, you can set up a pre-defined DOS command to do this with a single keystroke. At the prompt, press the following nine keys:

`[C] [O] [P] [Y] [Spacebar] [F10] [Spacebar] [A] [:]`

On the screen, you will see `COPY # A:` (The # symbol is shorthand for the current document name.) Now press [Enter]. Whenever you want to make a copy of the current document onto a floppy, you can do it with a single keystroke from the *DOS access* menu.

6.6.2   Other options in DOS access

F6 - *Erase a pre-defined DOS command*

This command allows you to clear any pre-defined DOS command. You will be prompted to press the function key of the command you want to erase.

F8 - *Save document before executing DOS command*

This command is a toggle. When on, it saves the current document to disk before starting the pre-defined DOS command, which eliminates the risk of your losing work while you are in DOS or any other program. And, by saving the current state of the document, it allows DOS to work with your most up-to-date version if you're using the current document option (**6.6.1**).

F9 - *Return to DOS temporarily*

This command allows you to return to DOS for more than a single command. After pressing [F9], you will go all the way to the DOS prompt. The reminder

```
Remember:  to return to Textra,
type EXIT at the DOS prompt
```

will appear. You can now type in DOS commands, run programs and batch files, etc., for as long as you want. When you want to return to *Norton Textra*, type **EXIT** at the DOS prompt, just as if it were a DOS command.

6.7   Customize   [Alt F6]

After you've become familiar with *Norton Textra* you may find that you don't like certain of the default settings. You may, for example, want to change the left and paragraph margins that *Norton Textra* will automatically use each time you create a new file. Or you may want to change the hardware options in order to fit the program to the computer you are using. You can change these settings each time you use the computer, or you can change them once: the *Customize* command allows you to modify *Norton Textra* to contain the default settings you want for all future work sessions and for all future documents you create.

Note, however, that some of your newly customized default settings will not change the settings in documents you have previously created (such as the left and right margins). Instead, *Norton Textra* will use the settings for that document that were saved with the document. You can change each of the settings in the old document and then save it; or you can retrieve the document, save it in ASCII format (see **9.9**); then retrieve it again with your customized version of *Norton Textra* – all switches and margins will reflect your new values.

6.7.1   The *Customize* menu

When you begin the *Customize* command, you will see the following menu:

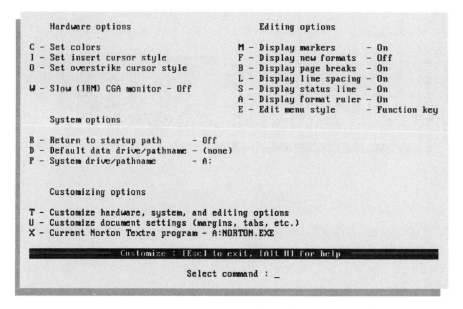

```
        Hardware options                    Editing options

C - Set colors                      M - Display markers        - On
I - Set insert cursor style         F - Display new formats    - Off
O - Set overstrike cursor style     B - Display page breaks    - On
                                    L - Display line spacing   - On
W - Slow (IBM) CGA monitor - Off    S - Display status line    - On
                                    A - Display format ruler   - On
                                    E - Edit menu style        - Function key
        System options

R - Return to startup path       - Off
D - Default data drive/pathname  - (none)
P - System drive/pathname        - A:


        Customizing options

T - Customize hardware, system, and editing options
U - Customize document settings (margins, tabs, etc.)
X - Current Norton Textra program - A:NORTON.EXE

============ Customize : [Esc] to exit, [Alt H] for help ============

                    Select command : _
```

6.7.2   Hardware options

C - *Set colors*

This command allows you to change how *Norton Textra* appears on the screen. With some of the IBM-compatible machines, you may need to play around with these options in order to have normal and highlighted text displayed distinctly.

When you begin this command, the following menu will appear (but note that the styles and fonts that are listed, like those in the *Highlighting* menu [**4.5.1**], will change depending on what printer you have selected in the *Print* menu [**8.3.1**]).

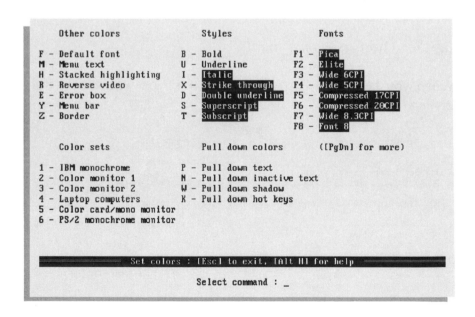

If you press any of the lettered options, you will be shown a chart with all the color or shading possibilities of your screen. You can use the left or right arrows to move across the chart and the up or down arrows to move vertically. When the color is the way you want that option to appear on your screen, press [Enter].

Setting cursor style

You may alter both the insert and the overstrike cursor styles from the *Customize* menu. When you press either [I] or [O], you will see the following boxed menu:

```
1 - Normal DOS cursor
2 - Half block
3 - Full block
4 - Split cursor

Select choice : _
```

(See **3.7** for a discussion of the difference between the insert and overstrike modes.)

W - Slow (IBM) CGA monitor

This command is a toggle that will only concern you if you have a CGA monitor running off an IBM display adaptor (or a fully compatible clone). On such a setup, *Norton Textra* may write too quickly to the screen, resulting in snow. If you're having such a problem, turn this toggle to on. Unfortunately, while this will clear up the problem of snow, it will also mean that the [PgUp] and [PgDn] commands will not work as quickly.

6.7.3   System options

R - Return to startup path

This toggle controls whether *Norton Textra* returns to where it was started from. If, after starting *Norton Textra*, you move around among different disk drives and/or subdirectories, you can turn this switch on and have *Norton Textra* return to the path it was started from or turn it off and remain wherever you are when you exit from *Norton Textra*.

D - Default data drive/pathname

This toggle allows you to select which disk drive *Norton Textra* searches for documents when you start up. If it is off, *Norton Textra* will look on the current drive. If you have a dual floppy disk system, you may want to turn this on and start *Norton Textra* from the A: drive and have it switch automatically to B: for your documents.

P - System drive/pathname

This is where *Norton Textra* looks for its system files, such as the help file (NORTON.HLP) or one of the dictionary files (see **4.7**). You probably won't need to change the setting since *Norton Textra* will assume that the system drive or path is the one from which it was started.

6.7.4 Customizing options

These options allow you to choose which of your changes you want to keep. If you press [T], all the current settings of options on this *Customize* menu as well as other settings (but not those for *Page layout*) will be saved to the current *Norton Textra* program; the next time you start *Norton Textra* the settings will be as you have changed them. If you press [U], all the current settings of options having to do with the layout or format of your document will be saved; the next time you create a document the settings will be as you have changed them.

Pressing [X] allows you to direct *Norton Textra* to your current *Textra* program (you won't need to do this if you are using DOS 3.0 or higher). You could also use this in order to have several versions of your basic *Norton Textra* program – one set up to work with a different printer, for example, or one with complicated formatting features for different documents you are working on.

6.7.5 Editing options

These toggles allow you to decide how much information about your current location in a document or about the formatting of a document *Norton Textra* will display. You can turn them off if you want a very blank screen.

[M]/Display markers will show onscreen markers indicating paragraphs (hard returns), forced page breaks, tabs, rulers, etc.

[F]/Display new formats will show onscreen where you have imbedded format rulers and what those rulers are.

[B]/Display page breaks will indicate where the pages of your document will break when it is printed out.

[L]/Display line spacing will show the line spacing as governed by the various rulers; text that is double-spaced, for instance, will appear double-spaced on the screen.

[S]/Display status line will show the status line at the top of the screen (**3.1**).

[A]/Display format ruler will show the format ruler indicating margins and tabs at the top of the screen.

[E]/Edit menu style toggles between three choices: traditional function key, new pull-down, and (none); this third option requires you to enter function key commands directly. (See chapter 10 for more on the pull-down menu.)

6.8   Comments   [Alt F7]

The *Comments* command can be used by you or by your instructor to insert comments in a document. While they will be attached to a particular place in your document and indicated by a special symbol, they will be separate from your document, so that you can still read or print out the document as if the comments weren't there.

Your instructor can use this command to mark your paper electronically with corrections, suggestions, or questions. But you also may find it useful as you read and critique your own work — "This argument can be stronger", "Didn't I find a good quote on this subject somewhere?" or "Double-check these dates."

When you begin the *Comments* command, you will see the following menu:

```
I - Insert hidden comment
B - Browse/edit comments
G - Generate
P - Print
```

If you press [I] to insert a comment, you will be taken to a comment window. Type the comment in. You are actually typing a little document, so you can enter whatever information you want, using *Norton Textra*'s normal editing features. Press [Esc] when you finish.

Press [B] from the *Comments* menu to browse or edit your comments. Press [G] to take all the information you have entered and generate a comment section at the end of the document, which can be edited like any other text.

If you want to print out your comments, press [P] from the *Comments* menu. When you print your document, you can print just the document itself or the document plus the comments (**8.4.2**).

6.9   Statistics   [Alt F8]

The *Statistics* command quickly gives you access to information about your file. It counts total pages, total lines, and total words, and tells you the current date and time (if your computer clock is accurate).

6.10   Endnotes   [Alt F9]

Although most academic papers are now documented using
parenthetical citations and an alphabetical list of works cited
(**6.5**), some instructors prefer to use superscript numbers in the
text leading to a numerical list of endnotes. Endnotes greatly
simplifies this task.

Advice is given within the *Online handbook* (**4.6.3**) for what
to cite and how to cite it in a paper; this command helps you
prepare the numerical endnotes that appear at the end of a
documented paper. You will enter the necessary information,
following the appropriate model given onscreen; *Norton Textra*
will format the information with the proper indent for the MLA
(Modern Language Association) alternative style and order the
notes numerically for you – even renumbering and reordering the
notes as necessary when you revise your paper.

When you begin the *Endnotes* command, you will see the
following menu:

```
I - Insert endnote
B - Browse/edit endnotes
G - Generate
P - Print
```

If you press [I] to insert a note, you will be taken to a new screen
with these instructions:

```
Type in the endnote, press [Esc] when you're finished
Press [F5] to see examples of other common formats
```

Below these instructions appears a sample work cited entry for a
book with one author, the format you will probably need most
often. If, however, the source you want to cite is of another
kind, press [F5] for a menu of examples. The samples will be
offered in MLA format.

Type the reference in, following the sample for spacing,
punctuation, capitalization, and specific information. Press [Esc]

when you have finished. *Norton Textra* will keep your endnotes properly formatted and ordered.

Press [B] from the *Endnotes* menu to browse or edit your notes. Press [G] to take all the information you have entered and generate an endnote section at the end of the document, which can be edited like any other text.

If you want to print out your endnotes, press [P]. When you print your document, you can print just the document itself or the document plus the endnotes (**8.4.2**).

Note that you can also use this command to type content notes – notes that further explain a point in your text. When you are inserting an endnote, you are actually typing in a little document, so you can enter whatever information you want, using *Norton Textra*'s normal editing features.

6.11   Options   [Alt F10]

Options provides a quick menu-driven alternative for certain commands that can also be used with [Ctrl] or [Alt] key combinations.

The *Options* menu offers six of these commands:

```
P - Page break        Ctrl P
F - Typing font       Ctrl F
T - Set tabs          Alt T
C - Center line       Alt C
R - Flush right line  Alt R
D - Current date      Alt D
```

From this menu you can press the letter key indicated to the left of each command. (Or at any time from the editor you can press the [Ctrl] or [Alt] key combination indicated at the right.)

[P]/Page break (or [Ctrl P] from the editor) forces a page break at the cursor position. Use this command if, for example, a chart or table is being divided between pages, or if a paragraph is being divided in an unattractive or confusing way.

[F]/Typing font (or [Ctrl F] from the editor) enables you to highlight text as you enter it (see **4.5.2**).

[T]/Set tabs (or [Alt T] from the editor) takes you to the *Modify/set tabs* menu (**7.3.6**).

[C]/Center line (or [Alt C] from the editor) centers the current line between the left and right margins. You will probably want to center the title of a paper, for example.

[R]/Flush right line (or [Alt R] from the editor) moves the current line so that it ends at the right margin.

[D]/Current date (or [Alt D] from the editor) inserts the current date at the current cursor position. This command reads the date from your computer's clock and inserts it in the form **November 20, 1992**. This is very useful when you are beginning a letter.

7

Formatting a Document

7.1   The *Page layout* menu   [Shift F8]

The *Page layout* command is used for defining the way your printed pages will look. This is where you choose the various margins (left, right, top, bottom), as well as features such as page numbering, paragraph style, headers and footers, and tabs.

When you start the *Page layout* command, the following menu will appear:

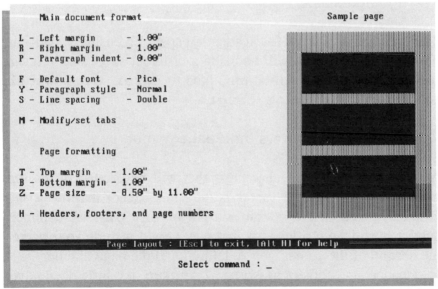

The sample page drawn on the right side of the screen gives you a rough idea of what your pages will look like, but keep in mind that it's only an approximation.

7.2   Page formatting

7.2.1   Top and bottom margins

These commands tell *Norton Textra* the amount of space (in inches) to leave blank at the top and bottom of each page. The header (if there is one) will be printed in the top margin and the footer (if there is one) will be printed in the bottom margin **(7.2.3)**.

Norton Textra* is set up with one-inch margins, based on the common 8½" x 11" sheet of paper. If you press [T] to change the top margin or [B] to change the bottom, you will be prompted to **Enter new value**. Enter the new value in inches and press [Enter].

7.2.2   Page size

The standard page size for academic papers or business letters is 8½" x 11", but if you will be using a different sheet size you can specify it here. You will be prompted to **Enter page width** and then to **Enter page length**.

7.2.3   Headers, footers, and page numbers

A header is a string of characters that will be printed in the top margin of each page; a footer is the same except that the string will be printed in the bottom margin of each page. A common header in college writing, for instance, would include your name, the section of the course you're taking, and the page number.

Headers and footers in *Norton Textra* are like little documents and can include as much information as you wish—they are limited only by the size of your margins. Just as when you're writing or editing documents, you'll be able to use all aspects of the editor when you're crafting headers and footers.

Headers, footers, page numbers menu

When you press [H] from the *Page layout* menu, you will reach the *Headers, footers, page numbers* menu:

```
    Headers

1 - Header style - Print same header on every page
2 - Header       - None


    Footers

4 - Footer style - Print same footer on every page
5 - Footer       - None


    Options

F - First page number to be printed - 1
N - Number of pages to skip          - 1



═══════ Headers, footers, page numbers : [Esc] to exit, [Alt H] for help ═══════

               Select command : _
```

Choosing header or footer style

These options toggle between **Print same header on every page** (or "same footer") and **Alternating**. Same *header* (or *footer*) is probably what you will use for most papers, as with name, course title, page number.

Alternating is useful with documents that, like books or magazines, are printed on both sides of the paper. Left-hand pages (even numbered pages) can have one header or footer, and right-hand pages (odd numbered pages) another.

If you have pressed [1] and created alternating headers or [4] and created alternating footers, the menu will now look a little different. The following is an example:

```
    Headers

1 - Header style  - Alternating
2 - Right page    - "# / FORMATTING A DOCUMENT"
3 - Left page     - "FORMATTING A DOCUMENT / #"


    Footers

4 - Footer style  - Alternating
5 - Right page    - None
6 - Left page     - "Norton Textra Writer 2.5"
```

You can mix styles—the header can be the same on every page, the footers alternating. You can have both headers and footers, one but not the other, or neither.

Entering headers or footers

When you press [2], [3], [5], or [6] to enter the headers or footers you want, you will be shown a new screen with the menu bar and the editing menu at the bottom, a formatting ruler in the middle above a blank area where the cursor is blinking, and the following instructions at the top:

```
· Type in the header, press [Esc] when you are finished...
· Press [Shift F1] to enter page number symbol
· Press [Alt C] to center a line
· Press [Alt R] to make a line flush right

· Press [Alt H] if you need some help
```

Enter whatever text you want to appear as your header or footer. Enter it and revise it just as you would any document.

If you want the page number to be a part of header or footer, press [Shift F1] where you want the page number to appear. The symbol # will appear on the screen. *Norton Textra* will insert the correct page number in place of the # when it prints the document.

Options

[F]/First page number to be printed allows you to begin numbering with a page number other than one. For example, if you are printing a document that is to follow another document that ends on page 39, you could tell *Norton Textra* that the first page number to be printed is 40.

When you press [F], *Norton Textra* will prompt you to **Enter first page number to be printed**.

[N]/Number of pages to skip allows you to treat a page or a number of pages at the beginning of your document differently from the rest. For example, you might want a title page or a contents page or a dedication. Or if you are printing a four-page business letter and want to put page numbers on every page after the first, you would tell *Norton Textra* to skip one page.

When you press [N], *Norton Textra* will prompt you to **Enter number of pages to skip**.

7.3   Document formatting

Note that you can change the settings of all these options for any of the formatting rulers in the *Edit formats* command (see **6.4**).

7.3.1 Left and right margins

These commands tell *Norton Textra* the left and right margins you want for the main document format.

Norton Textra is set up with one-inch margins, based on the common 8½" x 11" sheet of paper. If you press [L] to change the left margin or [R] to change the right, you will be prompted to **Enter new value**. Enter the new value in inches and press [Enter].

7.3.2   Paragraph indent

This command tells *Norton Textra* the paragraph indent you want for the main document format.

When you press [P], you will be prompted to **Enter new value**. Enter the new value in inches and press [Enter].

Each space on your screen is roughly equivalent to 0.1". For an indent of five spaces, enter 0.5". For a block paragraph (no indent), enter 0.0". For a hanging indent (in which the first line begins farther to the left than the following lines do), enter a negative value, such as -0.5".

7.3.3   Default font

This command leads to a font menu that will vary depending on the current printer (**8.3.1**). You can choose the font you want for the normal font of your document by pressing the letter indicated to its left in the menu.

7.3.4   Paragraph style

This command leads to a menu:

```
N - Normal (ragged right)
J - Justified
C - Centered
R - Flush right

     Select style : _
```

Press the key indicated next to the style you wish. With [N], lines will be even at the left margin but the right side will be ragged, with some lines longer and some shorter, as in a normal typed paper. [J] will line up both right and left margins. [C] will center all lines between the left and right margins. [R] will provide the opposite of [N]: lines will be even at the right margin but will be ragged at the left.

7.3.5 Line spacing

This command allows you to determine the line spacing you want. Pressing [S] will bring up the following menu:

```
S - Single spacing
0 - 1½ spacing
D - Double spacing
T - Triple spacing

Select spacing : _
```

Note that your text will be displayed with the line spacing you have selected if the *[L]/Display line spacing* option (**6.7.5**) is on in the *Customize* menu.

7.3.6 Modify/set tabs

When you press [M], the *Modify/set tabs* menu will appear at the bottom of your screen:

```
To set a tab, position the cursor, then press [T, C, D or R]....

T normal tab («)    D  decimal tab (o)  E  erase tab       M  move tab
C center tab (↔)    R  right tab   (»)  Q  erase all tabs  S  set exact tab
```

The symbols in parentheses will appear within your formatting rulers to show both the current location of tabs and which kind of tab each one is.

    Place the cursor where you want the tab to be and then press one of the four letter keys listed. [T] sets a normal tab; the left edges of text entered will line up at the tab. [D] sets a decimal tab; the decimal points in text entered will line up at the tab; this is useful for columns of figures. [C] sets a center tab; the center of text entered will line up at the tab. [R] sets a right tab; the right edges of text entered will line up at the tab.

You may instead want to set tabs the way you set margins (i.e., in inches), so that no matter what type font you use the tab location will be the same. Set an exact tab by pressing [S]. You will be prompted to choose whether the tab is to be normal, center, right, or decimal and then to **Enter value**.

7.4   Hard spaces and hyphens

Three other commands, although not part of the *Page layout* menu, help you shape the appearance of your text.

[Ctrl H]	Insert hard space
[Ctrl -]	Insert hard non-breaking hyphen
[Alt -]	Insert soft hyphen

When you press [Spacebar] to insert a blank space after a word, *Norton Textra* uses the spaces as a signal that it can break the line at that point if necessary: "Norton," for example, might end one line and "Textra" begin the next. You may want to keep certain characters or words together, however, even if there is a space between them. Instead of [Spacebar], press [Ctrl H] to insert a hard space; *Norton Textra* will not break the line at a hard space. "St. Louis," for example, may make more sense to your readers if kept on one line; the name of the French statesman de Gaulle would best be entered with a hard space.

When you press [-], you insert a *hard breaking hyphen*—the hyphen shows up on screen and *Norton Textra* will break the line immediately following the hyphen if necessary: "user-friendly," for example. But you may want to keep certain expressions together, even if they are hyphenated: phone numbers, for example. Press [Ctrl -] to insert a *hard non-breaking hyphen*.

If you find that certain very long words are making your right margin more ragged than you like, you can insert a *soft hyphen* by pressing [Alt -]. Such a hyphen will not show up unless the line is broken there; if you revise your text so that the word is now in the middle of the line, the soft hyphen will remain invisible.

8

Printing a Document

8.1   Print

The *Print* command is primarily used for printing documents. It can be used to decide which parts or how many copies of a document to print and to take advantage of your printer's capabilities for type styles and qualities.

You can quickly print a document without retrieving it first by pressing [F7] on the *Retrieve document* menu (**2.5.10**) or, after retrieving it, by pressing [P] on the *Main* menu (**3.2.3**). If you want to do anything other than print a single copy of the entire document as it is currently formatted, however, you will need to use the *Print* menu, which you reach by pressing [F7] on the *Shift* menu.

After you have pressed [Shift F7] or [F1][F7], the screen will clear, and the *Print* menu will appear:

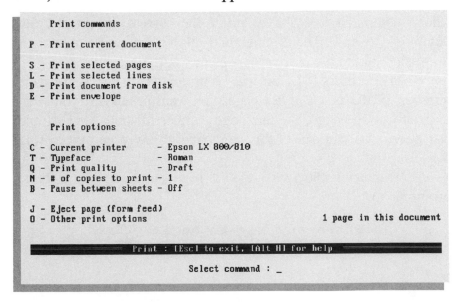

```
        Print commands

P - Print current document

S - Print selected pages
L - Print selected lines
D - Print document from disk
E - Print envelope


        Print options

C - Current printer       - Epson LX 800/810
T - Typeface              - Roman
Q - Print quality         - Draft
N - # of copies to print  - 1
B - Pause between sheets  - Off

J - Eject page (form feed)
O - Other print options                    1 page in this document


            Print : [Esc] to exit, [Alt H] for help

                Select command : _
```

Toward the lower right of your screen will be a line indicating the number of pages in the current document.

8.2   Print commands

8.2.1   *P - Print current document*

This is the most common printing option. When you press [P], the message

```
    Press any key to begin printing..._
    (Press [Esc] if you change your mind)
```

will appear. This gives you a chance to change your mind or to line up the paper in your printer. When you're ready to start printing, press any key on the keyboard. The current document will be printed using the current value of the *Page formatting* and *Print options*. Changing these after the file has begun printing will have no effect.

8.2.2   *S - Print selected pages*

The *P* command (see above) prints the current document from beginning to end. The *S* command allows you to print one or more pages from the current document.

When you press [S], you will be prompted, in order, for page numbers of the first and last pages you want printed. If you want to print just one page, use that page number for both the first and last page. You can cancel this command at any time by pressing the [Esc] key.

After entering the first and last page numbers, you will be prompted to

```
    Press any key to begin printing..._
    (Press [Esc] if you change your mind)
```

8.2.3 *L - Print selected lines*

This option allows you to print one or more lines from the current document. Page numbers, headers, and footers are ignored during this command. The lines are printed continuously, with no page breaks inserted.

After pressing [L], you will be placed back in the document so you can mark the lines that you want to be printed. You will be prompted to **Mark the text you want to print, then press [Enter]**... As you move the cursor up or down, the area you have marked will be highlighted so that you can see which lines will be printed.

You will then be asked to

> **Press any key to begin printing...**_
> **(Press [Esc] if you change your mind)**

8.2.4 *D - Print document from disk*

This option allows you to print a document from disk. You will be prompted to

> **Enter document name : _**

Enter the name of the document you want to print, then press [Enter]. If *Norton Textra* can't find the document, the message

> **Document not found**
> **Press the [Esc] key to continue...**

will appear. After pressing [Esc] you can try another document name.

You can print a document from any disk drive by prefixing the file name with the appropriate drive letter, as in

> **B:SAMPLE.LET**

If the document is found, *Norton Textra* will begin printing it. If the document was saved in Textra format, *Norton Textra* will use the values of the switches and margins that were saved with the document. If the document was saved in ASCII format, *Norton Textra* will use the current values shown in the *Print* menu. (See **9.9** for more information on Textra and ASCII formats.)

8.2.5   *E - Print envelope*

This command prompts you through the common task of printing a business envelope. After you have typed a business letter that includes the name and address of the addressee at the top of the letter, you can press [E] to reach the prompt to mark the first and last lines of the address. The *Envelope options* (**8.4.1**) in the *Other print options* menu allow you to specify the margins and type font you wish.

8.3   Print options

8.3.1   *C - Current printer*

Norton Textra is designed to take advantage of the capabilities of most printers. In order to best use its ability, you should make sure that the setting for current printer reflects the printer you will be using to print your document. Changing printers is easy, so if you will first be printing a draft on a dot-matrix printer, for example, and then printing the final version on a laser printer, you should in each case change the setting here to match the printer.

   When you press [C], you will be shown a list of *Printer families*. You should be able to find your printer on the list, but if your printer is not listed check your printer manual to see if the manufacturer claims compatibility with another, more widely used brand. When you find your printer family, or a compatible one, press the letter associated with it.

   You will then be shown a list of the *Printer models* within that family. Press the letter next to the model you will be using, or a compatible model.

Your printer is now installed. You will be asked

```
Would you like to install this
printer permanently ([Y]/[N]) ? _
```

If this printer is the one you will be using most often you will want to press [Y]. If you are just using it for a single document, you will want to press [N]. Whichever way you answer, *Norton Textra* always makes it easy for you to change the current printer setting.

8.3.2 *T - Typeface*

This switch is conditional—it will only appear on the *Print* menu if the *Current printer* you have selected supports different typefaces. The values that [T] toggles between depend on the particular printer.

8.3.3 *Q - Print quality*

This switch toggles between three options—draft, medium, and high. It is useful for dot-matrix printers that allow you to print quickly in draft mode or more slowly for a more polished look.

8.3.4 *N - # of copies to print*

This lets you print more than one copy of the file. If you choose this option, you will be prompted to

```
Enter new value (between 1 and 10000) : _
```

8.3.5 *B - Pause between sheets*

This allows you to use single sheets, such as letterhead, when printing documents. If this switch is on, every time *Norton Textra* finishes printing a page, you will be asked to

```
          Insert new sheet,
    then press any key to resume..._
```

After inserting and aligning the next sheet, press any key on the keyboard to resume printing, or press [Esc] if you want to cancel the rest of the printing.

If this switch is off, *Norton Textra* will continue, page after page, until it finishes with the file or you tell it to stop, by pressing [F1] (to pause) or [Esc] (to cancel). This is fine for printers that use tractor feed and continuous form paper.

8.3.6 *Eject page (form feed)*

[J] sends a form feed character to your printer and the current page will be ejected.

8.4　Other print options

Pressing [O] from the *Print* menu leads to the *Other print options* menu:

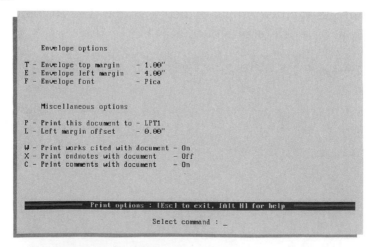

```
        Envelope options

T - Envelope top margin    - 1.00"
E - Envelope left margin   - 4.00"
F - Envelope font          - Pica


        Miscellaneous options

P - Print this document to - LPT1
L - Left margin offset     - 0.00"

W - Print works cited with document - On
X - Print endnotes with document    - Off
C - Print comments with document    - On



========= Print options : [Esc] to exit, [Alt H] for help =========

                Select command : _
```

8.4.1   Envelope options

The *Envelope options* allow you to set the margins and the type font you wish to use in printing an envelope (see **8.2.5**). After pressing [T] or [E], enter the desired margin in inches. [F] leads to a font menu offering the font options of the current printer (see **8.3.1**).

8.4.2 Miscellaneous options

P - Print this document to

This command lets you select which printer port *Norton Textra* will print to. In almost all cases this will be LPT1. When you select [P], you will see the following choices:

```
1 - LPT1     (parallel)
2 - LPT2
3 - LPT3
4 - COM1     (serial)
5 - COM2
6 - COM3
7 - COM4
8 - Disk file

Select choice : _
```

If you select one of the serial ports (4−7),you will have a chance to set up the various parameters that control serial printing, such as baud rate, parity, etc. You should consult the manual that comes with your printer in order to find out the values for these parameters.

If you select [8], *Disk file*, you will be prompted to **Enter filename**. This command allows you to print to disk as if the disk were a printer—pagebreaks, headers, and footers will be in place.

L - Left margin offset

This allows you to add a specified number of spaces to each printed line, effectively shifting it to the right. This allows you to compensate for the way different printers print text, without having to reformat your documents.

W - Print works cited with document

This allows you to decide whether you want to print just the main part of your document (as you might if you want to print a draft) or if you want to print the document and the list of works cited (**6.5**).

X - Print endnotes with document

This allows you to decide whether you want to print just the main part of your document (as you might if you want to print a draft) or if you want to print the document and all its endnotes (**6.10**).

H - Print hidden comments with document

This allows you to decide whether you want to print just the main part of your document or if you want to print the document and all the attached hidden comments (**6.8**), whether written by you, your instructor, or someone else.

9

Saving or Exiting a Document

9.1   Saving and exiting

The work that you do in any session at the keyboard exists only in the current memory of the computer until you save it to disk. Before you exit a document, then, you will want to save your work. In addition, if you work for a long time on the same document, you should save your work every fifteen minutes or so, to prevent any surge in electrical power or other problem from erasing all your efforts.

You will most often save a document by pressing [S] in the *Main* menu (**3.2.3**). You can also save from the *Save options* menu (**9.2**).

Exiting a document is to leave it—to close a file—whether or not you have saved it first. Exiting without saving is also called abandoning.

9.2 The Save options menu   [Shift F10]

After starting the *Save options* command, the screen will clear, and the following menu will appear:

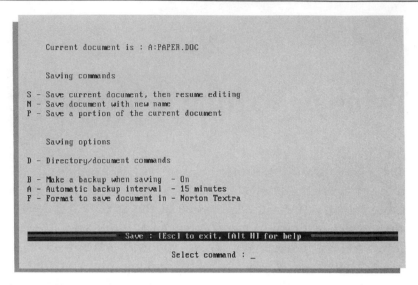

```
Current document is : A:PAPER.DOC


Saving commands

S - Save current document, then resume editing
N - Save document with new name
P - Save a portion of the current document


Saving options

D - Directory/document commands

B - Make a backup when saving  - On
A - Automatic backup interval  - 15 minutes
F - Format to save document in - Norton Textra


════════════════ Save : [Esc] to exit, [Alt H] for help ════════════════

                     Select command : _
```

9.3   Save current document, then resume editing

This option is designed for periodically backing up your work. Saving your work every 15-20 minutes is a good habit to develop. This means that you will never lose more than 15 minutes of work if your computer is accidentally turned off or there is a problem with your electrical lines.

Note that *Norton Textra* has a command that allows you to specify an automatic backup interval (**9.8**).

9.4   Save document with new name

This option lets you save the current document with a new name. You will be prompted:

Enter filename : _

Press [Esc] if you change your mind, and you can then choose another option. Otherwise, type in the new name you want to give the document. You cannot use a name you've already used on that disk (but you can use the same filename with a different extension; see **2.4**). If you type in the name of a file that already exists, you will see the following prompt:

There is already a document named

XXXX.XXX

Do you want to overwrite it ?
([Y] or [N], [Esc] to cancel)

The [N] option can also be used for saving your work onto another disk. If the current disk drive is A:, and you want to save your work onto the B: disk drive, type **B:** in front of the name you want to give the document. For example:

b:newname.doc

9.5   Save a portion of the current document

This command allows you to mark a group of lines and then save those lines into a new document.

When you press [P] to start this command, *Norton Textra* will prompt you to mark the text you want to save to disk. When you have done this, *Norton Textra* will prompt you to

Enter filename : _

After you have typed in the name of the new document, *Norton Textra* will save the text you marked in a file of that name.

9.6   Directory/document commands

This command leads to the *Directory/document commands* menu, which offers the same options as the *Retrieve document* menu (**2.5.1**). You can use this command, for example, to see how much free space is available on your disk.

9.7   Make a backup when saving

This switch controls whether *Norton Textra* makes a backup copy of your original document when you save the current version to disk. If it's off, no backup copy will be made when you save your work to disk. The main advantage of this is that it saves disk space, since there aren't two copies of each document on the disk. The disadvantage, of course, is that if the original is somehow destroyed, there isn't a backup copy on the disk. If you're diligent about making your own backup copies of working disks, this risk can be minimized.

9.8   Automatic backup interval

With *Automatic backup interval* on, *Norton Textra* will keep track of how much time has gone by since the last time your work was saved to disk. After the backup interval elapses, your current work will automatically be saved to disk. This is an excellent way to prevent disasters from happening.

When you turn this switch on, *Norton Textra* will prompt you to

```
Enter backup interval, in minutes (between 1 and 60)
```

Automatic backup interval won't save your document unless you've made changes.

9.9   Format to save document in

This command activates a menu that gives you a choice of four formats to save your document in: Norton Textra, Hard ASCII, Soft ASCII, and Word Perfect 5.x. (ASCII is pronounced *ass-key*, from American Standard Code for Information Interchange).

A document saved in Textra format contains a complete history of where you are within the current document. When you retrieve the document the next time, everything will be exactly as you left it: the cursor will be in the same place, the tabs and margins will be the same, etc.

If you save in either Hard or Soft ASCII format, none of this information is saved. When you retrieve the document, the margins and switches will have the default values—the values *Norton Textra* uses when you create a new document.

Unlike Soft ASCII, Hard ASCII preserves the document's lineation by placing "hard returns" at the end of each line.

Use the ASCII formats if you are transmitting files or reading your files in some other software.

The Word Perfect 5.x format saves your document so that it may be read by *Word Perfect 5.x*. *Norton Textra* can also read *Word Perfect 5.x* files (see **2.5.15**).

You will normally want to save in Norton Textra format, and you may never want to change this toggle.

10

Working with Pull-Down Menus and a Mouse

10.1   Two new features

Norton Textra 2.5 has two exciting new features: an alternative set of pull-down menus that largely replace the traditional function key menus described in the previous chapters, and support for a mouse to move the cursor, block text, and control most editing functions. In general, these two features are designed to be used together: mouse users will presumably use the pull-down menus, while users without a mouse will stay with the traditional function key menus. However, as will be described below, the two features work independently of each other: you can use the pull-down menus without a mouse, and you can use the function key menus with one.

10.2   Pull-down menus

This section briefly describes how to use the pull-down menus. (See section **6.7.5** for information on how to select them instead of the traditional function key menus.)

The word processing functions arranged in three sets of function keys in the traditional menu are now grouped into six large headings—*File*, *Edit*, *Format*, *Insert*, *Options*, and *Handbook*, each of which is listed as a selection on the *pull-down menu bar* located at the top of the edit screen.

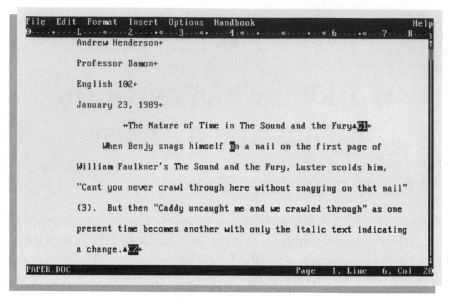

10.3 Using the pull-down menus without a mouse

To activate the main pull-down menus without a mouse, hold down the [Alt] key and press the highlighted letter for each option: [F] for *File*; [E] for *Edit*; [M] for *Format*; [I] for *Insert*; [O] for *Options*; and [A] for *Handbook*. For example, pressing [Alt F] will activate the *File* sub-menu, producing the following screen:

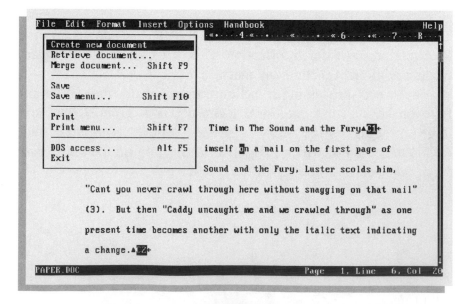

To activate selections from a sub-menu, either press the highlighted key or use the up and down arrows to highlight the desired option and press [Enter]. For example, to activate the *Print menu* from the *File* sub-menu, press [I] or press [Down arrow] until the highlight bar covers *Print menu* and press [Enter].

10.4   Using the pull-down menus with a mouse

To activate the main pull-down menus with a mouse, move the mouse pointer (a small, gray rectangle) so that it is over any part of one of the six options and click once on the left button of a two-button right-hand mouse. This will cause the sub-menu to pop down over the edit screen. (See example in **10.3** above.)

It's easy to browse the menu options if you're looking for a particular selection but don't know where to find it. Just click and hold on one of the six options. A sub-menu will pop down. Without releasing the button, move to the left or right. Each sub-menu will pop down in succession. Release the button when you find the menu you want.

To activate selections from a sub-menu, move the mouse so that the highlight bar is over the desired option and click once.

10.5   Scrolling with a mouse

Moving the cursor on the current screen using a mouse is completely intuitive: move the mouse pointer to where you want the cursor and click once on the left button.

To move above or below the current screen, you have to use the *scroll bar* on the right-hand edge of the screen in one of the following ways:

To scroll up or down one line at a time, click once on the up or down arrow at either end of the scroll bar.

To scroll up or down continuously, click-and-hold on the up or down arrow at either end of the scroll bar.

To page up or page down, click once on the scroll bar either above or below the notched area (known as the *thumb*).

To scroll quickly forward or back in the entire text, click-and-hold on the thumb and drag it up or down to the desired location in the document—note that in clicking-and-dragging the thumb you need not worry about staying on the rail.

10.6   Editing with a mouse

Many people find that block operations like *copying* and *moving* are easier with a mouse. Either of these operations follows the same two- or three-step sequence.

First, click-and-hold at the start (or the end) of the text you want to alter, dragging the mouse to the end (or the beginning) of the block before letting up on the button; second, select the function you want to perform, ordinarily by activating the pull-down menu as explained in **10.4** above; and third (for copying or moving text), move the mouse pointer to the desired new location and click once to reposition the cursor and double-click to copy or move the text.

You can also *delete* with a mouse by clicking-and-dragging to mark the text block to be deleted, and then either activating the *Edit* pull-down menu or more directly by pressing either the [Del] or [Backspace] keys.

Three other mouse features: Double-clicking on a word blocks it, while single-clicking unblocks any blocked text; the click-and-drag technique can be used at the tab menu to reset tabs and margins; and pressing the right button at any time acts as [Esc].

You can also use the mouse in any of the *Norton Textra* menus (such as the *Retrieve*, the *Print*, *Page layout* menu) or even with the regular function key menus at the bottom of the editing screen merely by clicking on the desired option.

10.7   Using a mouse with the function key menu

Norton Textra allows you to use a mouse with the function key menu. For example, to access the *Save options* menu, place the mouse pointer over **F1 more ...** and click the left button until the *Shift menu* appears. Click once on any part of the **F10 Save options** selection.

Once inside the *Save options* menu you can activate any of the options on the screen by placing the mouse pointer over the selection and clicking once.

Remember, the right mouse button works exactly like the [Esc] key.

10.8   Buttons

Norton Textra allows you to use your mouse to activate onscreen *buttons* — bracketed keystroke abbreviations that perform the same function as keyboard keys. Common buttons include [Enter], [Esc], [PgDn], and [PgUp]. To activate a button, place the mouse pointer within the brackets and click once.

A

Error messages

This appendix lists the error messages in *Norton Textra*. Under most circumstances, error messages are displayed in the center of the screen, inside a box. Some require you to press [Esc] to continue. Others allow you the option of pressing [F1] to get more information. If you press [F1], *Norton Textra* will attempt to find the extended error message inside the TEXTRA.HLP file and display it on the screen.

Bad command or file name

This is an error message from DOS which means that DOS couldn't find the NORTON.EXE file when you typed **norton** to start it up. Look at the contents of the disk (using the DOS DIR command), to see exactly what is on the disk. Recopy *Norton Textra* onto the disk if necessary, or replace the disk with a *Norton Textra* program disk.

If you're using a hard disk, either switch to a subdirectory that contains *Norton Textra* or, if you're familiar with the DOS PATH command, create a PATH that points to the subdirectory where *Norton Textra* is stored (see your DOS manual for more information).

Cannot copy a file onto itself

This message will occur in the *Copy* command (**2.5.9**) if the source and destination filenames are the same.

Cannot find temporary files created by Merge - replace original disk

This message occurs during the *Merge/browse* command (**5.8**) if *Norton Textra* cannot find the temporary files it created before retrieving the second file. It usually indicates that some disk swapping has gone on since you've initiated the *Merge/browse* command.

Can't open a subdirectory

This message will appear if you type the name of a subdirectory at the **Enter document name or number :** prompt in the *Retrieve document* menu. To switch to that subdirectory, type its number in the onscreen directory or use the CD or CHDIR commands (**B.2**).

Can't split this window here

Each window must be at least seven columns wide and one line high. (At the bottom of the screen, the minimum height will be somewhat different, depending on the way the editing menu is set up.) This error message will appear if you attempt to make a horizontal split in a window of minimum height or a vertical split in a window of minimum width.

Changes have been made to
      xxxxx.xxx
Do you want to save it first ?
([Y] or [N], [Esc] to cancel)

This warning message will appear if you've made some changes to the current document, and you then select an option other than *Save* in the *Main* menu. It warns you that the changes you've made to the current document will be lost unless you save them first. Press [Y] to save the changes, [N] to let the changes go, or [Esc] to cancel this command.

Current disk is full.

This message can appear any time *Norton Textra* is writing a file (as in the *Copy* or *Save* commands, or saving with auto backup or saving the supplemental dictionary). The extended error message discusses this situation in more detail.

Current Textra program not found

This error message can appear when you are trying to customize *Norton Textra* (**6.7**). If you are using DOS 3.0 or higher, you should never have a problem; if you are using an earlier DOS, you may have to help *Norton Textra* by pressing [X] and indicating the current Textra program (the EXE file that you booted at the beginning of your work session, with drive letter and any pathname): A:NORTON, for example.

Disk error reading
Abort, Retry, or Ignore?

This message can appear when you are trying to load *Norton Textra* and indicates that there is a problem with the disk or disk drive. If you're using a backup copy of *Norton Textra*, try the original disk. If you're just starting out and haven't had a chance to make a backup yet, see **1.3.4**.

Document not found

This message is displayed any time (with one exception; see **Document wasn't found** below) you try to retrieve a document and *Norton Textra* can't find it. Usually, this means that you've mistyped the name of the document.

Document wasn't found.
Do you want to create it ([Y] or [N]) ?

This message is displayed if you try to retrieve a document that doesn't exist in the *Retrieve document* menu (**2.5.1**) or if you use the shortcut for creating a document (**2.5.4**).

Documents cannot be saved
with a .BAK extension

You cannot save a document with a .BAK extension. *Norton Textra* will prompt you to rename the document; you may use any legal filename and extension (see **2.4**) except for the extension BAK.

Error creating document (directory full, read-only filename, or illegal pathname)

This error is very uncommon and this message is unlikely to ever appear. Conceivably, it could occur in any operation when a document is created (as in *Copy*, *Create*, *Save*, or in saving the supplemental dictionary). Do note that you cannot have more than 112 files on the root directory of a floppy disk or 512 on the root directory of a fixed disk.

Error deleting document

This only occurs when you are using the *Delete* command (**2.5.11**) and have entered the name of a subdirectory rather than a document.

Error opening/creating document (no handles available)

The circumstances that could lead to the appearance of this error message are nearly inconceivable. For example, you would need to have booted several memory-resident programs, all doing input/output at once, and then while editing a document to ask *Norton Textra* for one of the films-on-disk from a help screen. Should you see this message, you can remedy the problem by returning to DOS and using EDLIN to raise the value of FILES= within the CONFIG.SYS file–to 10 or 20, for example. Consult your DOS manual for more information on EDLIN and CONFIG.SYS.

Error renaming document

This only occurs when you are using the *Rename* command (**2.5.12**). Either you are trying to rename a directory or you have used illegal characters in the new filename (**2.4**).

Illegal dictionary

This will only appear if you are using the *Spell check* command (**4.7**). It indicates that the dictionary has somehow been corrupted. Recopy the dictionary from your original disk.

Illegal disk drive

You get this message if you try to select a disk drive that doesn't exist on your system.

Illegal document name

This message occurs when you type an illegal filename (**2.4**) when selecting a file.

Illegal help file

This message indicates that the help file wasn't in the form *Norton Textra* expected. This could occur if the help file has somehow been corrupted. Recopy the help file from your original program disk.

Illegal print driver file

This message will only appear in the *Current printer* sequence (**8.3.1**). It indicates that the print driver has somehow been corrupted. Recopy PRINTERS.DRV from your original disk.

Non-System disk or disk error
Replace and strike any key when ready

This DOS message means that you're trying to start up your computer with the *Norton Textra* program disk. You need to start your computer with a DOS disk (**1.2**).

Not enough memory . . .

These words begin ten error messages, such as **Not enough memory to check spelling, Not enough memory** to load (or create) this document, and Not enough memory to merge this text. The memory referred to is the available memory of the computer you are using. (See Program too big . . . below for an explanation of available memory.)

Pathname not found

This message will occur if you type in the name of a subdirectory that doesn't exist.

Program too big to fit in memory

This DOS error message will occur if there isn't enough available memory in your system to load *Norton Textra*.

Although we say that *Norton Textra* can be run on 256K machines, it actually uses approximately 200K of memory in addition to the area set aside for your text (which can vary in size, the minimum being 20K). In a 256K machine, however, DOS 2.0 takes up close to 30K. Subsequent versions of DOS take up even more. (There are numerous ways to take up even more memory, with memory-resident programs such as RAM disks, print spoolers, and programs such as *Sidekick*. In addition, if you have a file called CONFIG.SYS on your DOS disk, it can contain instructions that take up memory as well.)

What really matters is how much free space you have. You can determine this by using the DOS command CHKDSK, which, in addition to giving you information about the current disk drive, tells you how much total memory there is and how much of that memory is free (expressed as bytes free). There must be approximately 200,000 bytes free in order for *Norton Textra* to load.

Required Textra file not found:
xxxxxxxx

This message will appear any time *Norton Textra* cannot find one of its system files:

NORTON.HLP, FILM.HLP, HANDBOOK.HLP, MAIN.WRD, FREQUENT.WRD, or PRINTERS.DRV. Use the *System drive/pathname* command (**6.7.3**) to point *Norton Textra* to the right place.

> **The block you've marked is too big to be copied**

Depending on how much memory you have and how full your document is, there are limitations on how large a block can be copied or moved. (Note that the *Merge/browse* command is, in effect, a *Copy block* command, and the same restrictions apply.)

> **The disk drive isn't responding. Is the door fully closed?**

This message is equivalent to the DOS error message:

> **Disk error reading drive n**
> **Abort, Retry, or Ignore?**

It means that the disk drive wasn't responding correctly when *Norton Textra* tried to read from (or write to) it. It could mean that the disk drive door isn't fully closed, a connecting cable is loose, a board inside the computer is loose, or that the disk or disk drive itself has failed.

> **The extended error messages are not available**

This will appear if you request more information (by pressing [F1] from the error box prompt) and *Norton Textra* cannot find NORTON.HLP.

> **There is already a document named**
> **xxxxx.xxx.**
> **Do you want to overwrite it ? ([Y] or [N])**

This can happen in the *[N]/Save document with new name command* (**9.4**) or *[P]/Save a portion of the current document* command (**9.5**).

> **There's not enough room to move the block you've marked**

See **The block you've marked is too big to be copied.**

> **This document is marked read-only.**
> **It needs a new name to be saved.**

This will appear if you attempt to save a read-only file from the *Main* menu. (Read-only is a DOS attribute you can give to files to protect them from accidental deletion or modification; see your DOS manual.) Instead, you must use *[N]/Save document with new name* from the *Save options* menu (**9.4**).

> **This disk is unformatted (replace with a formatted disk and try again)**

You cannot use a disk straight from the box. You must format it first (see **B.3.6**).

> **This disk is write-protected (which means documents can't be saved onto it).**

This message means that the disk in the current disk drive is write-protected. If you're using a 5¼" disk, the notch that normally appears near the upper right part of the disk (the write-protect notch) is covered; peel off the write-protect sticker. If you're using a 3½" disk, the little plastic switch in the upper right corner needs to be moved the other way. Hard disks also occasionally contain write protect switches.

> **This citation is full.**
> **This footer is full**
> **This header is full**

Norton Textra allocates a certain amount of memory, separate from your current document, for works cited and for headers and footers. These error messages indicate that no more memory is available for the feature named. There may still, however, be enough memory to continue editing your document.

This document is full. You must delete some text before adding more.

This message means that you've reached *Norton Textra*'s upper limit on document size, based on how much memory your computer has available. You can either delete some text from the current document or divide the document into two, each containing a portion of the current document.

This document is unnamed, and needs to be named before saving.

While you can create and edit an unnamed document, you must name it in order to save it.

Too many tabs set; you must clear some before setting more.

This message will appear if, in the *Set tabs* command, you press [T] to set a tab when there are already twenty set.

Too many windows, can't split any more

You are limited to eight windows; this message indicates that you must close an existing window before you can create a new one.

Unable to load (because there's not enough memory) or find COMMAND.COM

This message may appear with low-memory machines when you are using the DOS access command (**6.6**).

Unreadable Textra program

This message may appear in the *Customize* menu (**6.7**). It probably indicates that you have made a mistake in entering *[X]/Current Textra program*.

Waiting for printer

This message will appear if *Norton Textra* tries to send a character to the printer and there's no response. This error could mean that there's a problem with the physical connection between the printer and the computer (a cable is loose, for example), or it could mean that the wrong printer port has been selected (see **8.4.2**).

Wild cards not allowed in destination

The *Copy* command (**2.5.9**) accepts only a subdirectory or filename for a destination. Global filename characters (**2.5.14**), or wildcards, are not accepted.

B

A DOS PRIMER

DOS is short for Disk Operating System and is most commonly pronounced as a single word rhyming with "moss." DOS is the program you use to start your computer.

B.1 Loading DOS

On many computers, after you start them with DOS, you will be prompted to enter the date and time:

```
Current date is   xxxxxxxxxx
Enter new date (mm-dd-yy) :

Current time is   xxxxxxxxxx
Enter new time :
```

Other systems automatically keep track of the date and time, and this step is skipped.

After that, the DOS prompt will appear. The DOS prompt is a signal that you can begin typing DOS commands or loading other software programs. The most common DOS prompt is A> _, although it's possible that your DOS prompt looks a little different.

B.2 DOS and your disk drives

In addition to being a signal that DOS is ready to begin accepting commands, the DOS prompt tells you which disk drive is the default disk drive (or default drive). The default disk drive is where DOS will look for documents or programs.

Each disk drive on the computer is assigned a letter. If your computer has two floppy disk drives, one will be **A:** (usually the one on the left, or the one on top), and the other is **B:**. If your computer has one floppy disk drive and one hard disk drive, the floppy drive is usually **A:** and the hard disk drive is usually **C:**. Unfortunately, there is such a wide variety of computer systems that its impossible to include all possible configurations here.

You can switch disk drives (or change the default disk drive) by typing the letter, then a colon, then pressing [Enter]. For example, with the DOS prompt on the screen, you can switch to the **B:** disk drive (if you have one) by typing **B:** and then pressing [Enter]. A new DOS prompt, B>_ will appear, indicating that **B:** is the default disk drive.

You can switch sub-directories by typing CD (or CHDIR) followed by a backslash and the sub-directory name. You can reach the root directory by typing CD (or CHDIR) followed by a backslash. In either case, then press [Enter].

B.3   Some important DOS commands

Some of the most commonly used DOS commands are discussed here; for more information see your DOS manual. In the examples, we will use upper case letters, but you can use any combination of upper and lower case letters when typing DOS commands.

B.3.1   CHKDSK

CHKDSK (CheckDisk) is actually two commands in one: it gives you a report on the disk in the current disk drive (or the current subdirectory). It will report such things as the number of files, how much space they take up, how much free space is left on the disk, etc.

It also tells you two important pieces of information on the computer memory in your system: how much memory is installed in your system, and how much of it is free (available memory).

B.3.2   COPY

COPY is used to make an identical copy of a document. If from the **A:** drive you want to make a copy of a document named QUARTER4.RPT onto a disk in the **B:** disk drive, you would type at the DOS prompt

        COPY QUARTER4.RPT B:

and then press [Enter]. DOS will then read QUARTER4.RPT from the A disk drive and make a copy of it onto the disk in the B disk drive. The copy will have the same name as the original document.

Note that you can also use a different name for the copy:

        COPY QUARTER4.RPT B:DISASTER.RPT

You should use COPY frequently to make backup copies of important documents onto disks that you then store safely in a separate area from your day-to-day work disks.

B.3.3   DEL, ERASE

These are the DOS commands for erasing (deleting, removing) files from a floppy disk. If you had a file called REPORT.BAK on your disk, you could erase it by typing at the DOS prompt

        ERASE REPORT.BAK

You could delete every backup file (all files ending with .BAK) by typing at the DOS prompt

        ERASE *.BAK

B.3.4   DIR

DIR (short for Directory) is used for getting a list of the files (documents) on a disk.

B.3.5   DISKCOPY

DISKCOPY is used for making an exact duplicate of one disk onto an-other. DISKCOPY has the FORMAT command (see **B.3.6**) built into it, so you don't have to FORMAT a blank disk before using DISKCOPY.

Section **1.3** has a detailed description of how to use the DISKCOPY command to make an exact copy of your *Norton Textra* program disk. It's also a good way to make a backup copy of any disk with important information.

B.3.6   FORMAT

When a disk is brand-new (fresh out of the box), it's unformatted, which means that most DOS commands will be unable to read it. If you attempt to do a DIR of an unformatted disk, for example, you will see the DOS error message:

> **Disk error reading xxxxx**
> **Abort, Retry, or Ignore?**

FORMAT prepares blank disks for use with DOS. To format a disk in the **B:** disk drive, type at the DOS prompt

> **FORMAT B:**

DOS will respond by asking you to

> **Insert new diskette for drive B:**
> **and strike any key when ready_**

This gives you a chance to change your mind (press [Ctrl C] to cancel the operation). Note that you can format any disk—even a disk that is already formatted with information on it. But keep in mind that formatting a disk wipes out everything on it, so be sure there aren't any files you want to keep.

B.3.7   RENAME

RENAME changes the name of a document. If you have a document named REPORT.BAK on your disk, and you want to change the name to QUARTER4.RPT, at the DOS prompt, type

RENAME REPORT.BAK QUARTER4.RPT

and then press [Enter].

INDEX

NORTON TEXTRA WRITER 2.5 REGISTRATION FORM

Fill out and return this page—not a photocopy—in order to register your purchase of NORTON TEXTRA WRITER. Registration entitles you to the following:

- A periodic newsletter describing the enhancements and revisions planned for NORTON TEXTRA WRITER and associated software.

- A reduced price—for registrants only—on software revisions and enhancements for a period of four years from the date of registration.

- Immediate replacement of defective NORTON TEXTRA WRITER disks returned to W. W. Norton (you must return the original disk, not a copy).

Please print:

_____
NAME

_____
SCHOOL

_____
PERMANENT ADDRESS

_____

_____
CITY   STATE or Province   ZIP or Postal Code

( ) STUDENT   ( ) INSTRUCTOR   ( ) LAB COORDINATOR   ( ) OTHER

Please check one:
( ) STAND-ALONE ONLINE HANDBOOK
( ) ONLINE HANDBOOK TO ACCOMPANY *THE CONFIDENT WRITER*
( ) ONLINE HANDBOOK TO ACCOMPANY *THE NORTON GUIDE TO WRITING*
( ) ONLINE HANDBOOK TO ACCOMPANY *WRITING: A COLLEGE HANDBOOK*

Please check one:
( ) 5.25" DISKS
( ) 3.5" DISK

Mail to:

NORTON TEXTRA WRITER
W. W. Norton & Company, Inc.
500 Fifth Avenue
New York, NY 10110